URBAN TRAVEL GUIDE
SAN FRANCISCO

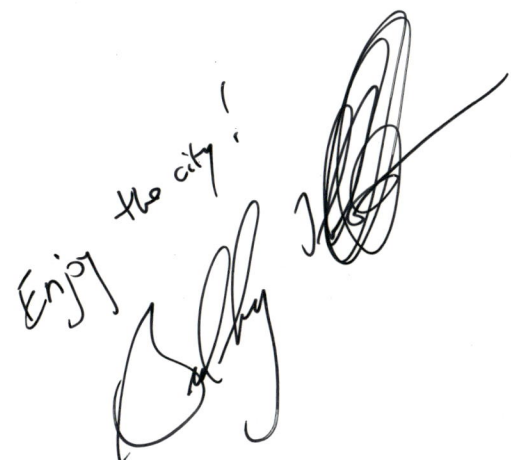

urban travel guide san francisco   ISBN 90 5767 126 3
© mo' media, breda, the netherlands, 2004.
All rights reserved. No part of this guide may be reproduced, stored in a retrieval system or made public in any form or by any means, electronic, mechanical or otherwise, without the prior written permission of the publisher.

COLOPHON

AUTHOR bradley charbonneau **FINAL EDITING** zahra sethna **PHOTOGRAPHY** rebecca dadson **GRAPHIC DESIGN** mattmo concept | design, amsterdam **CARTOGRAPHY** eurocartografie, hendrik-ido-ambacht **PROJECT GUIDANCE** joyce enthoven & marty van rijen, mo' media

This guide has been compiled with the utmost care. Mo' Media BV cannot be held liable in the case of any inaccuracies within the text. Any remarks or comments should be directed to the following address.

mo' media, attn. mo'guides, p.o. box 7028, 4800 ga, breda, the netherlands,
e-mail info@momedia.nl

PREFACE

"Finally! A guidebook even a local could use!" was the comment I heard most while doing this guidebook. Whether you were born here or have never been here, I hope you'll feel right at home in San Francisco with this guide.

Each chapter has a different theme with a distinct perspective on the city. **The Whole World Lives in San Francisco** chapter leads you into the intimate world of cultures that each call this city home. **Body, Mind, & Soul** helps you to understand the organically grown, über-health conscious, your-body-is-your-temple lifestyle of Northern California. **Sophisticate** shows off the finest and funkiest of the artists, designers, writers and architects. From weekend-ending Monday morning raves to Sunday morning at church, **Swinging San Francisco** gives you at least a week's worth of rhythm and groove. There's so much happening in **The Valencia Corridor**, hurry up and get over there to see what's newer than tomorrow and hipper than thou. **Hayes Valley** is a neighborhood where you stand and point: coffee here, new shoes there, hair done here — then you say to yourself, "This would be a place I'd like to live." Step back into the recent history of the city with **Bohemia, California**. Finally, go hang out with the young and the beautiful in **The Marina Triangle**.

Bradley Charbonneau

Bradley Charbonneau stood on a corner several years ago and said, "I'd like to live here." He has ever since.

Photographer Rebecca Dadson captured the inside, outside, and underside of San Francisco as only someone who fell in love with the city could.

CONTENTS

3	PREFACE
5	HOW TO USE THIS GUIDE
6	PRACTICAL INFORMATION
8	THE WHOLE WORLD LIVES IN SAN FRANCISCO
44	BODY, MIND & SOUL
72	SOPHISTICATE
104	SWINGING SAN FRANCISCO
126	THE VALENCIA CORRIDOR
144	HAYES VALLEY
166	BOHEMIA, CALIFORNIA
186	THE MARINA TRIANGLE
208	MAPS
218	CATEGORY INDEX
220	ALPHABETICAL INDEX

HOW TO USE THIS GUIDE

In this guide we list the best addresses in San Francisco for shopping, dining and drinking, as well as nightlife, lodging, culture and other sights of interest. Each address has a number; you'll find these numbers both on the map at the beginning of each chapter and on the detailed maps at the end of the guide. For each address, a letter indicates on which detailed map you can find it. The number on the maps corresponds to the page number of the address (in the example below, Encantada would be on page 14). We've also used colors to indicate the different categories:

- 🟢 shopping
- 🟠 food & drink
- 🔴 nightlife
- 🟡 lodging
- 🟣 culture
- 🔵 various

EXAMPLE: NUMBER 14, MAP G ENCANTADA
You can find the address of Encantada on the map at the beginning of 'The whole world lives in San Francisco' and on the more detailed map G at the end of the guide. Number 14 is green, which means this is a shop.

PRICE INDICATION FOR HOTELS AND RESTAURANTS
The prices listed are average prices for entrées (main course) in restaurants, cocktails in bars, etc. For hotels, the price listed is the starting rate for a double room per night but keep in mind that this is the published rate – with a few mouse clicks or phone calls, you should be able to get a better rate.

PHONE NUMBERS
All phone numbers are in the 415 area code, unless otherwise noted.

DO YOU HAVE ANY SUGGESTIONS FOR US?
We've tried to compile this guide with the utmost care. However, addresses change, prices go up and phone numbers get disconnected. Should you no longer be able to find a certain address or have other comments or suggestions for us concerning this guide, please let us know. You'll find our address in the colophon on page 2 of the book.

PRACTICAL INFORMATION

You've been for a ride on the cable car and strolled down Fisherman's Wharf. So, are you ready for the real San Francisco? There are people who have lived in this city for years and have never been to Pier 39. Now that you've got it out of your system, you're that much closer to seeing the real city.

A good place to start
San Francisco Visitor Information Center, 900 Market Street (in Halladie Plaza at Market and Fifth Streets near Union Square), TELEPHONE (415) 391-2000, WEBSITE www.sfvisitor.org

MUNI
Get a MUNI map at the visitor's center – this will save you time, headaches and hours of wondering. The city's public transportation system is split up into buses, streetcars, cable cars and trams. It makes life a lot simpler if you buy a pass for a few days, a week, or even a month, depending on how long you're staying. That way, you won't have to worry about having correct change or your transfer expiring. You can also view and purchase MUNI maps by logging on to www.sfmuni.com. A single fare, valid for as far as you can go in 90 minutes, is $1.25 or $0.35 if you're between the ages of 5-17 or 65+. Monthly passes are $45 or $10 for 5-17 and 65+. Weekly passes are $12 for every age group. The lettered lines are the electric streetcars (J, K, etc.) and trams (F). Buses are numbered (38, 42, etc.). An "L" after a bus number denotes "Limited" service, which means the bus does not make all stops. Some lines also have late-night service (see the map).

Taxi
Getting a cab in San Francisco can be a challenge. Your best bet is to wait at one of the larger hotels, such as the Westin St. Francis and the Marriott. Or call one of the following taxi companies:
De Soto 673-1414
Luxor 282-4141
Veteran's 552-1300
Yellow Cab 626-2345

Tickets
For half price theater tickets on the day of the performance, check out the TIX BAY AREA kiosk on Union Square: www.theatrebayarea.org, 433-7827 OPENING HOURS tue-thu 11:00am-6:00pm, fri-sat 11:00am-7:00pm. Other possibilities: BASS, charge-by-phone 510 762-2277, www.ticketmaster.com or www.tickets.com.

Public holidays
New Year's Day, January 1
Martin Luther King Day, 3rd Monday January
President's Day, 3rd Monday February
Memorial Day, last Monday May
Independence Day, July 4

Labor Day, first Monday September
Columbus Day, 2nd Monday October
Election Day, first Tuesday November
Veterans Day, November 11
Thanksgiving Day, 4th Thursday November
Christmas Day, December 25

San Francisco festivities
Chinese New Year, usually early February
St. Patrick's Day Parade, Sunday nearest March 17
Bay to Breakers, Sunday late May
Cinco de Mayo, May 5
Carnaval SF, last weekend May
Lesbian and Gay Pride Day, Sunday late June
Fleet Week, early October
Halloween, October 31
Day of the Dead, November 2

Useful websites
www.sfvisitor.org (visitor's center)
www.sfgate.com (local, regional news)
www.sfstation.com (arts & entertainment)
www.sfweekly.com (arts & entertainment)
www.sfbg.com (arts & entertainment)

Newspapers & magazines
SF Chronicle (main local newspaper)
SF Magazine (local living, news, events)
SF Weekly (news, arts, entertainment, music)
SF Bay Guardian (news, culture, arts, entertainment)
7x7 (magazine, what's new and innovative)

Festivals
SF INTERNATIONAL FILM FESTIVAL (www.sfiff.org), 2-week festival in April-May.

STERN GROVE FESTIVAL (www.sterngrove.org), your chance to see the San Francisco Symphony or the San Francisco Ballet for free on a Sunday afternoon in June, July and August.

SHAKESPEARE IN THE PARK (www.sfshakes.org), you can catch your yearly dose of Shakespeare in Golden Gate Park on Saturdays and Sundays around Labor Day time.

SF JAZZ FESTIVAL (www.sfjazz.org), every year in late October – early November in different venues around the city.

shopping　　food & drink　　nightlife　　lodging　　culture　　various

THE WHOLE WORLD LIVES IN SAN FRANCISCO

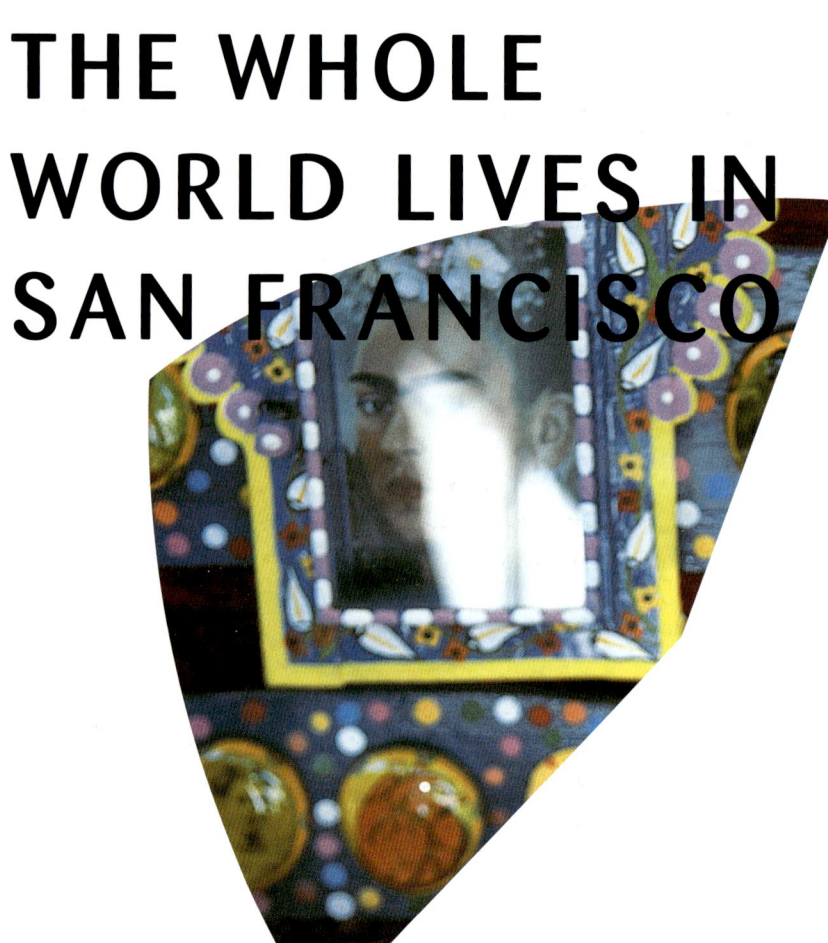

shopping   food & drink   nightlife   lodging   culture   various

Chinatown = Chinese. North Beach = Italians. Mission = Latinos. Downtown = everyone. San Francisco is not a big city – only roughly seven square miles – but you can walk through countries and even continents in an afternoon here.

As evidence, most street signs and bank machines in **Chinatown** are written in Mandarin. Many of the shops in the **Mission district** are exclusively in Spanish. When you walk around **Union Square** and hear languages such as German, Tagalog, Dutch and Vietnamese, don't assume those people are tourists. Old men in **North Beach** still play cards and mumble in Italian. The Indians and Pakistanis in the **Tenderloin's** restaurants are there because the food is just like back home. (A good test of a restaurant's authenticity is always the number of "locals" who eat there. If locals don't go, the food might be good but it's probably not very authentic.) There are usually two versions of a neighborhood: one for locals and one for tourists. When you get off the tourist track, you'll enter another world.

Stroll through **North Beach** and try to imagine it at the turn of the last century. Business was booming from the California gold rush and silver from Nevada, and the place was hopping. Fifty years later, the **Beatniks** roamed the streets, promoting their "politics of dissent" and free love. This has always been a bustling part of town and things haven't really changed that much over the years, with jazz festivals, lively nightclubs and your choice of dozens of Italian restaurants still readily available. Tourists now have the run of **Columbus Avenue**, but the Italians and the Beats are still there; they're just hidden away. To slow down and watch it all happen, grab some picnic supplies at Molinari's Deli and relax on the grass at **Washington Square.**

As you make your way through the little alleyways of **Chinatown**, keep your eyes, ears and nose open for details – they are everywhere. Listen closely and you might hear women playing mah-jongg behind closed doors. If you manage to hear them, close your eyes and it'll be hard to believe you're not in China. Maybe you'll stumble on a fortune cookie factory hidden down a back alley. Get off Grant Avenue (south of Columbus is Chinatown, north is North Beach) and go one street west to **Stockton** (especially on a Saturday morning) for the real deal. Crowds of local Chinese do their grocery shopping here and you can hardly walk down the sidewalk because it's so crowded (you may have an easier time walking in the street but watch out for the buses!) You'll see everything from turtles and frogs to ginseng and bok choy – and those are just the items you'll recognize. If you're hesitant to buy a root that's said to prolong life or a frog that's still hopping, lunchtime is a good time to go to the **House of Nanking**, when you're more likely to get a seat than at dinner.

From the hustle and bustle of Chinatown, head towards the **TransAmerica** building, at the heart of the **Financial District**. Find **Belden Place** and you'll discover an alley between the skyscrapers that was seemingly **transported from Paris**. Treat yourself to a cocktail and listen to the languages of French, finesse and finance. You're sitting in the business center of San Francisco. During the week, the streets are bustling with business people in suits, cell phones galore and a "got-to-run-catch-you-later-I'll-call-you" attitude.

shopping   food & drink   nightlife   lodging   culture   various

Walk on towards **Union Square** and you'll enter a world shared by tourists, cable cars, Macy's and many of the city's locals. Most of the buildings around Union Square are apartments, but rarely are they larger than two-bedroom units so there are few families living downtown. Young singles, recent transplants to the city and a variety of **nationalities** make downtown a vibrant place to live – if you can put up with garbage day being every single day of the week. Locals who live downtown know that they'll never have to go more than a few blocks to find Indian, Pakistani, Burmese, Indonesian, French, Vietnamese, Italian, Thai or Chinese food, plus a selection of American-style diners. Be wary, however, of restaurants that try to do too much: "Best American Hamburger and Chinese Food to Go" seems like a stretch.

Farther south is the **Mission district**, where you'll enter a world of Latino culture. There are immigrants here from Mexico, Peru, Guatemala, Spain and many other countries. Walk along Valencia Street, also known as the **Valencia Corridor**, for furniture shops, bookstores and endless restaurants or head to **Mission Street**, one street east, which is a real taste of Mexico and "la vida Latina" with its authentic "taquerias", 99-cent stores, thrift shops and some of the city's hottest bars and clubs. ¿No hablas Español? No problemo.

If you'd like to get an insider's view on the many sides of the city, **City Guides** does fantastic tours of many parts of town. They'll tell you stories that only locals could know. This is a great way to get more out of a walk around the city. Tours are offered all over town, at all hours of the day, all year round.

THE WHOLE WORLD LIVES IN SAN FRANCISCO

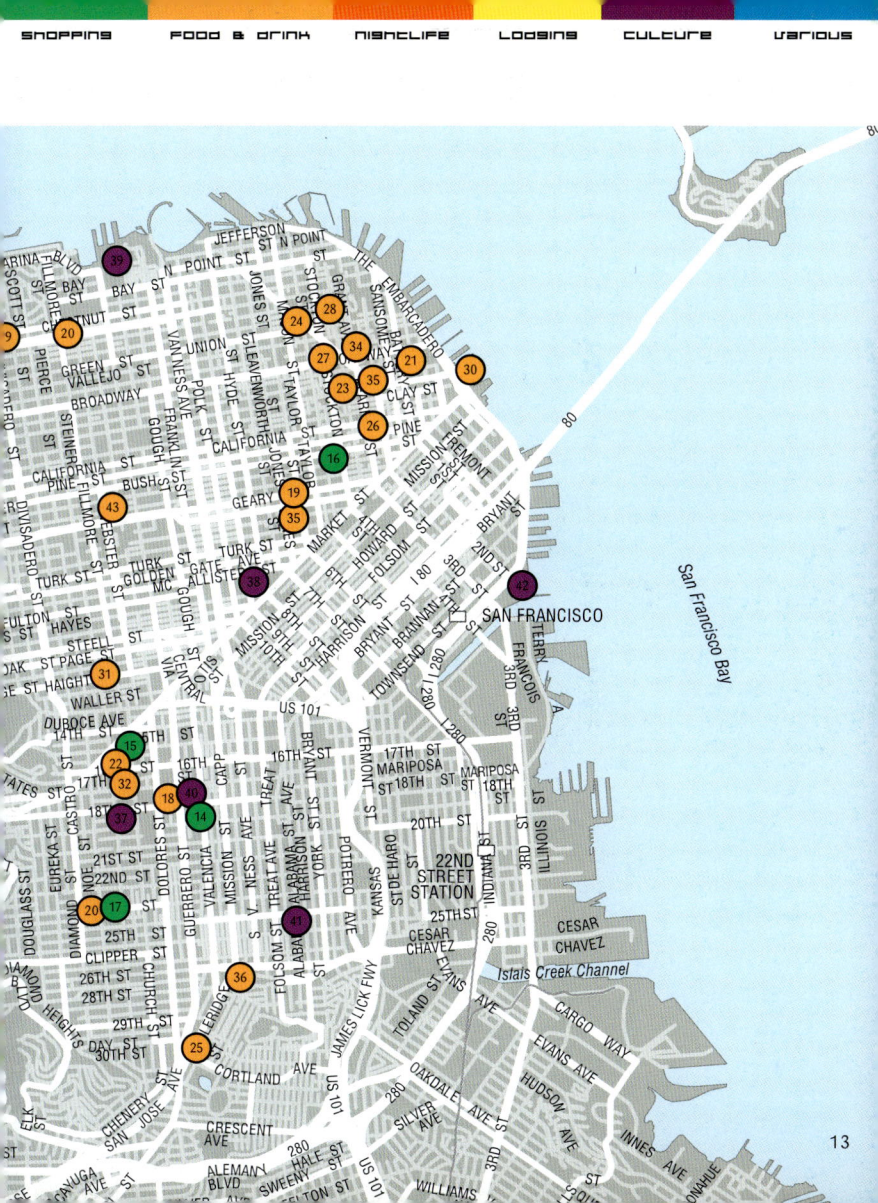

ENCANTADA number 14 map G

ADDRESS 904 valencia @ 20th street **TELEPHONE** 642-3939 **OPENING HOURS** tue-thu,sun 12pm-6pm, fri-sat 12pm-8pm **CREDIT CARDS** visa, mastercard **MUNI** 14, 26, j

Bowls and pitchers, pottery and sculpture, cards and magnets – Encantada has it all in pure Mexican style and with loads of color. Frida Kahlo tote bags and beautifully hand crafted pewter salad spoons with tile inlays seem hidden, as if this were a Mexican artist's tasteful attic. Through the open door is the art gallery, where there are revolving shows and seasonal exhibitions, such as for the Day of the Dead and Christmas.

There are many places in town where you can get Indonesian wood furniture, but at The Barking Frog the pieces have that something extra. There are large items, such as beds, chairs, dressers, and trunks, but also keep an eye out for the small stuff. Around Christmas, the store carries hand-made, hand-painted Christmas ornaments shaped like brightly colored fish decked out in fruit-basket hats. The items in this store are so unique and irresistible, you'll find yourself inventing friends to buy them for – might as well admit it, you really want them for yourself!

number 15 map G # THE BARKING FROG

ADDRESS 2215 market @ sanchez **TELEPHONE** 436-9600 **WEBSITE** www.thebarkingfrog.com **OPENING HOURS** daily 11am-7pm **CREDIT CARDS** visa, mastercard, amex **MUNI** 24, 35, 37, f

In Europe, Mickey Mouse, Charlie Brown and Dennis the Menace aren't nearly as popular as Tintin, Babar and Asterix. At Kar'ikter, you can discover what all the fuss is about. You'll also encounter Euro-designed thermoses, colorful kitchenware and gifts so unique you might not know what to do with them. Get ready for hidden treasures like the Lomo camera, which takes four pictures at once, using regular film. Next door is Alessi (424 sutter), where you can get ultra-cool Italian watches, glassware, silverware and plastic ware.

KAR'IKTER number 16 map D

ADDRESS 418 sutter @ stockton **TELEPHONE** 434-1120 **WEBSITE** www.karikter.com **OPENING HOURS** mon-sat 10am-7pm, sun 11am-5pm **CREDIT CARDS** visa, mastercard, amex **MUNI** 2, 3, 4, 30, 38, 45

shopping   food & drink   nightlife   lodging   culture   various

ADDRESS 4018 24th street @ noe **TELEPHONE** 648-8068 **WEBSITE** www.globalexchange.org **OPENING HOURS** sun-fri 11am-7pm, sat 10am-7pm **CREDIT CARDS** visa, mastercard, amex **MUNI** 24, 48, j

number 17 map G # GLOBAL EXCHANGE

Global Exchange is more than just a store selling exotic trinkets; it's a human rights organization that makes sure the Balinese artisan who hand-crafted those pearl drop silver earrings is going to get her fair share of the income. The organization also offers "Reality Tours" which, compared to TV's reality shows, are actually real. These educational tours give travelers an inside look into the realities of life in developing countries. Step inside this shop and be transported to another world – both literally and figuratively.

PLATANOS number 18 map G

ADDRESS 598 guerrero @ 18th street **TELEPHONE** 252-9281 **WEBSITE** www.platanos-sf.com **OPENING HOURS** sun-mon, wed-thu 5:30pm-11pm, fri-sat 10am-2:30pm, 5:30pm-11:30pm **CREDIT CARDS** visa, mastercard **PRICE** $14 **MUNI** 14, 26, 33, 49, j

Achiote-marinated pork with mango and papaya is undeniably a dish from south of the border, but the question at Platanos is, which border? Most of the dishes come from Honduras, Nicaragua, El Salvador and Mexico and all of them are fresh and tasty. Try the Spanish paella with Mexican chorizo or Mexican "chiles rellenos" with French brie.

The close quarters at Dottie's make the home cooking taste even better. On Sunday mornings around 11am, just as church services at Glide are ending, a line of serious Sunday brunchers starts to form. Every last crumb of muffin, scone and bread here is baked from scratch on the premises. If you come with a big party and there aren't enough seats inside for all of you, you'll have to face one of the world's most difficult ethical questions: whether friendship is more important than a crunchy blueberry-cornmeal pancake topped with butter and syrup.

number 19 map C

DOTTIE'S TRUE BLUE CAFE

ADDRESS 522 jones @ geary **TELEPHONE** 885-2767 **OPENING HOURS** thu-mon 7:30am-3pm **CREDIT CARDS** visa, mastercard **PRICE** $6 **MUNI** 2, 3, 4, 27, 38

Chicken burgers, guacamole burgers, pesto burgers, China burgers… You might have to come in and taste some of these concoctions to truly appreciate them. The fact that the milkshakes are made with Dreyer's ice cream is enough to make this worth a visit – sip one slowly on the front patio on 24th street or the back patio on Steiner. The choice of homemade sauces, garden burgers, turkey burgers and tofu burgers might make your head spin. If so, be safe and go with a Barney's Burger. You won't be disappointed.

BARNEY'S GOURMET HAMBURGERS

number 20 map B, C, G

ADDRESS two locations (1) 3344 steiner @ chestnut (2) 4138 24th street @ castro **TELEPHONE** 563-0307; 282-7770 **WEBSITE** www.barneysrestaurant.com **OPENING HOURS** (1) mon-thu 11am-10:30pm, fri-sat 11am-11pm, sun 11am-9:30pm (2) daily 11am-9:30pm **CREDIT CARDS** visa, mastercard **PRICE** $6 **MUNI** (1) 22, 28, 30, 43 (2) 24, 48

KOKKARI ESTIATORIO
number 21 map D

ADDRESS 200 jackson @ front **TELEPHONE** 981-0983 **WEBSITE** www.kokkari.com **OPENING HOURS** mon-fri 11:30am-2:30pm, mon-thu 5:30pm-10pm, fri-sat 5:30-11pm, taverna menu (bar snacks) mon-fri 2:30pm-5:30pm **CREDIT CARDS** visa, mastercard, amex **PRICE** $18 **MUNI** 12, 83

This is no blue-and-white souvlaki shack; this is fine Greek dining. Soft beige walls, thick wood beams and wrought iron chandeliers surround you, while the open kitchen will make you wish you had a rich Greek uncle with a rustic summer home like this. The ambiance gets you in the door, but the lamb chops will make you come back again. While you're here, explore the little known Jackson Square district, with its red brick buildings set against the backdrop of the towering financial district.

There's a guy who comes to Tin Pan five times a week, every week, and orders the same thing every time: red curry. He's either a connoisseur or a fanatic ... or maybe a bit of both. To his credit, however, the curry does have heaps of shrimp, silky coconut, tasty cilantro and just enough kick to keep things interesting. Try a Tin Pan pilsner to help cool things down and use chopsticks to slow down your intake speed or it will all be gone before you know what happened.

TIN PAN number 22 map G

ADDRESS 2251 market @ noe **TELEPHONE** 565-0733 **WEBSITE** www.tinpansf.com **OPENING HOURS** fri-sat 11am-midnight, sun-thu 11am-11pm **CREDIT CARDS** visa, mastercard, amex **PRICE** $10 **MUNI** 24, 35, 37, f, k, l, m

number 23 map D # HOUSE OF NANKING

ADDRESS 919 kearny @ columbus **TELEPHONE** 421-1429 **OPENING HOURS** mon-sat 12pm-10pm, sun 4pm-10pm **CREDIT CARDS** none **PRICE** $8 **MUNI** 12, 15, 30, 45

There are at least a dozen Chinese restaurants within a stone's throw of this place, but on any given night, this one is packed and the others are not. What gives? Taste. This restaurant manages to pack a punch of taste into every meal. There are so many rave reviews on the walls they've almost become wallpaper. The waiters know what's fresh so don't bother ordering from the menu. Just mention the ingredients you like – chicken, beef, pork, seafood or vegetables – and let the kitchen staff work its magic.

With homemade bread and desserts and a menu that changes with the chef's mood, Da Flora is like being a guest in an Italian home (one with a dash of Hungarian). If it weren't for MUNI bus 30 cruising by every once in a while, you could lose yourself and dream that you were drifting along the romantic canals of Venice. As a wise man once whispered, "This isn't cooking, it's alchemy."

ADDRESS 701 columbus @ filbert **TELEPHONE** 981-4664 **OPENING HOURS** tue-sat 5:30pm-9:30pm
CREDIT CARDS visa, mastercard **PRICE** $15 **MUNI** 15, 30, 41, 45

DA FLORA number 24 map D

ADDRESS 3489 mission @ cortland **TELEPHONE** 821-3949 **WEBSITE** www.zantespizza.com **OPENING HOURS** daily 11am-3pm, 5pm-11pm **CREDIT CARDS** visa, mastercard, amex **PRICE** $9 **MUNI** 14, 24, 26, 67, j

ZANTE PIZZA & INDIAN CUISINE

number 25 map p. 13

Replace tomato sauce with a light, delicious curry and the usual pepperoni and mushrooms with spinach, eggplant, tandoori chicken and cilantro and you've got yourself a slice of Indian heaven. Just walk in and order "the best Indian pizza". Rumor has it there's other food on the menu too, but you don't need to know about that. What you do need to know is that Zante delivers. If they won't come as far as your hotel, charter a helicopter, do anything, but get that pizza.

BELDEN PLACE number 26 map D

ADDRESS belden place, bush @ kearny **TELEPHONE** (1) 986-5673 (2) 986-6491 (3) 986-6287 (4) 433-5200
WEBSITE www.beldenplace.com **OPENING HOURS** various **CREDIT CARDS** mostly visa, mastercard **PRICE** $18
MUNI 9, 15

Hidden between the skyscrapers of the financial district, Belden Place is a cozy alley that feels like Paris. The grilled rack of lamb at (1) Café Bastille is juicy and tender and served with sweet potatoes. (2) Plouf is famous for its daily fresh mussel specials with a choice of six different sauces. At (3) b44, a Catalan bistro, try the hearty paella with chorizo, chicken, shrimp, mussels, clams and more. At the end of the alley is (4) Café 52, with its ever-popular Café Combo of chicken, prawns and crab cakes.

This is a tiny place, just a single aisle of goods, but what goods they are: wines, cheeses, breads, and sausages. What else does one need? Pick out a few fresh rolls from the bread bin and a nice bottle of red wine or two, then turn (slowly) towards the glass showcase. Salamis lie next to pepperonis, ham and turkey, just calling out to be on your sandwich. Cheeses, fresh and gooey or hard and sharp, sit locked up forlornly behind the glass beckoning to be freed. Pick up some olives dripping with oil, fresh salads or delicious finger-foods and try not to drool on the glass. Be warned, Molinari's is closed on Sundays.

number 27 map D **MOLINARI DELICATESSEN**

ADDRESS 373 columbus @ vallejo **TELEPHONE** 421-2337 **WEBSITE** www.molinarideli.com **OPENING HOURS** mon-fri 8am-6pm, sat 7:30am-5:30pm **CREDIT CARDS** visa, mastercard **PRICE** $5 **MUNI** 15, 30, 45

Liguria's menu is simple. In fact, it's so simple it's as if half of it fell off. Focaccia is all they do. Life is near utopia for the owners: do what you love, when you want and when the focaccia's gone, it's gone for the day. This place is a neighborhood favorite, and so is Mario's Bohemian cigar store, which serves cappuccino and makes delicious sandwiches with Liguria's focaccia (566 columbus @ union, open 10am-11pm).

LIGURIA BAKERY number 28 map D

ADDRESS 1700 stockton@ filbert **TELEPHONE** 421-3786 **OPENING HOURS** mon-fri 8am-2pm, sat 7am-2pm, sun 7am-12pm **CREDIT CARDS** none **PRICE** $3 **MUNI** 15, 30, 39, 45, powell/mason cable car

shopping　　food & drink　　nightlife　　lodging　　culture　　various

number 29 map B, C # CAFÉ MARIMBA

ADDRESS 2317 chestnut @ divisadero **TELEPHONE** 776-1506 **OPENING HOURS** mon 5:30pm-10pm, sun, tue-thu 11:30am-10pm, fri-sat 11:30am-11pm **CREDIT CARDS** visa, mastercard, amex **PRICE** $18 **MUNI** 28, 30, 43,

This is not Tex-Mex, this is real Oaxacan-style Mexican cooking; the guacamole is tangy and the margaritas bite back. From the homemade tortillas to the mole and salsas, this food is fresh. You won't be the only one loving the food here, so definitely make a reservation.

THE SLANTED DOOR number 30 map D

ADDRESS ferry building, embarcadero @ market **TELEPHONE** 861-8032 **WEBSITE** www.slanteddoor.com
OPENING HOURS check website for latest **CREDIT CARDS** visa, mastercard **PRICE** $17 **MUNI** 2, 6, 7, 9, 14, 21, 31, 32, 66, 71, f, j, k, l, m, n, bart: embarcadero

The Slanted Door's new location in the Ferry Building gives it something it never had before: a view. The open and airy restaurant is right next to the water with a wide view of the bay, the bridge and the boats. While you're staring off into the beyond, try the cubed filet mignon, called "shaking beef", or the chicken simmered in caramel sauce.

At Indian Oven you'll hear the constant murmur of chatting, hungry people waiting in the front for a table every single night. You can watch the cooks in the open kitchen as they skillfully prepare tandoori chicken, calamari curry or "jheenga masala," huge prawns sauteed in a tangy sauce of tomatoes and spices. If things heat up too much, cool down with a tall bottle of Taj Mahal beer and smile at the crowds waiting outside.

number 31 map G **INDIAN OVEN**

ADDRESS 233 fillmore @ haight **TELEPHONE** 626-1628 **OPENING HOURS** daily 5pm-11pm **CREDIT CARDS** visa, mastercard, amex **PRICE** $12 **MUNI** 6, 7, 22, 37, 66, 71, j, n

Off the busy main drag of Market Street, you can step into a neighborhood eatery that lives up to its name – and you'll know it when you enter. There's a huge basket of tangerines at the front of the bar and the back brick wall is painted a happy orange. The orange colors, coupled with the large palms and the classic white, evoke exotic visions of Asia. The food is vibrant too: salmon with mango salad, tangerine Thai shrimp and rosemary chicken kabob are just a few of the fusion-style dishes available. Try the special sake cocktail, the Tangerita.

TANGERINE number 32 map G

ADDRESS 3499 16th street @ sanchez **TELEPHONE** 626-1700 **WEBSITE** www.tangerinesf.com **OPENING HOURS** daily 11am-3pm, 5pm-10pm, sat-sun brunch 10am-3pm **CREDIT CARDS** visa, mastercard, amex **PRICE** $12 **MUNI** 22, 37, f, j, k, l, m

number 33 map A **TON KIANG**

ADDRESS 5821 geary @ 23rd avenue **TELEPHONE** 387-8273 **WEBSITE** www.tonkiang.com **OPENING HOURS** mon-fri 10am-10pm, sat 9:30am-10:30pm, sun 9am-10pm **CREDIT CARDS** visa, mastercard, amex **PRICE** nine items for two people $30 **MUNI** 2, 38

Bring everyone you know (make reservations), get a big, round table and get ready for a culinary adventure. Don't worry if you don't understand what the staff is offering you – they probably don't understand you either, unless you speak Mandarin. Just choose the dim sum delights that don't scare you too much and wash them down with some hot tea or fresh Tsingtao Chinese brew. This has been a local dim sum favorite for years.

THE HELMAND number 34 map D

ADDRESS 430 broadway @ kearny **TELEPHONE** 362-0641 **OPENING HOURS** daily 5:30pm-10:30pm **CREDIT CARDS** visa, mastercard, amex **PRICE** $17 **MUNI** 12, 15, 30, 45

The Helmand is a nice way to escape from the crowds at many of the North Beach Italian restaurants. You won't find tomato paste and meatballs here. Instead, try "kaddo borawni" (pan-fried pumpkin with sugar and yogurt) or the "bowlani" (pastry shells filled with leeks or potatoes). Equally delicious is the "sabzi challow", a spinach stew with lamb served on Basmati rice. You can't get much more authentic than this: the owner is none other than Mahmoud Karzai, the brother of Afghanistan's president Hamid Karzai.

Loud Indian music and flowing, multi-colored fabrics give the impression of being in an exotic bazaar. This restaurant doesn't have a liquor license, so be sure to bring your own beer or wine. Once you settle in with a cup of sweet, milky tea, plan on staying a while so you can enjoy every bite without overwhelming your taste buds. Although, at these prices there's no reason why you can't come back again and again.

number 35 map C, D, E **NAAN 'N CURRY**

ADDRESS three locations (1) 478 o'farrell @ jones (2) 533 jackson @ kearny (3) 642 irving @ 7th avenue
TELEPHONE 775-1349 **OPENING HOURS** daily 12pm-12am **CREDIT CARDS** none **PRICE** $6 **MUNI** (1) 27, 38 (2) 12, 15, (3) 6, 43, 44, n

shopping   food & drink   nightlife   lodging   culture   various

Art students and yuppies, lesbian party girls and swinging salsa singles – El Rio truly is for everyone. This is a place where you can be yourself – what or whoever that may be – and feel totally at home. Free oysters and world beat music on Fridays, salsa on Sundays and Wednesdays and dollar drinks on Mondays are some more reasons to go. Head out to the patio to cool down when things get too hot on the dance floor.

ADDRESS 3158 mission @ valencia **TELEPHONE** 282-3325 **WEBSITE** www.elriosf.com **OPENING HOURS** (may vary by season) mon 3pm-midnight, tue-sun 3pm-2am **CREDIT CARDS** none **PRICE** $3-8 cover on weekends **MUNI** 12, 14, 26, 49, 67 bart: 24th street

EL RIO   number 36 map G

ADDRESS 3895 18th street @ sanchez **TELEPHONE** 621-8135 **WEBSITE** www.karmamoffett.com **OPENING HOURS** fri-sun evenings 8pm, rsvp **CREDIT CARDS** none **PRICE** $15 **MUNI** 24, 33, 35, j

KARMA MOFFETT'S TIBETAN BELL CEREMONY

number 37 map G

The art, jewelry and musical instruments in this gallery are all beautiful to look at, but the real reason to come is to hear Karma's recital. A symbolic journey to Tibet, Karma plays instruments ranging from the Native American flute to a Tibetan longhorn, bowls and bells, and finally the Tingsha and conch shells that bring you to your destination and then slowly and rhythmically back again. He has perfected the art of circular breathing, thus allowing him to hold a note for several minutes. This should definitely soothe your soul …

Italian architect Gae Aulenti transformed a Parisian train station into the Musée d'Orsay and now has transformed the old San Francisco main library into the Asian Art Museum. Somehow this massive structure manages to be intimate and private. Travel through India, Vietnam, ancient Japan and China while moving through lightness and near darkness, open expanses and cozy corridors. Take the free audio tour to get some insight into what you'll see, but don't even think about trying to see the whole thing. Just enjoy what you can and see the rest next time.

ASIAN ART MUSEUM number 38 map C

ADDRESS 200 larkin @ mcallister **TELEPHONE** 581-3500 **WEBSITE** www.asianart.org **OPENING HOURS** tue-sun 10am-5pm, thu 10am-9pm **CREDIT CARDS** visa, mastercard, amex **PRICE** $10 **MUNI** 5, 6, 7, 9, 19, 21, f, j, k, l, m, n, bart: civic center

number 39 map C **FORT MASON**

ADDRESS buchanan @ marina blvd. **TELEPHONE** 441-3400 **WEBSITE** www.fortmason.org **OPENING HOURS** various **MUNI** 10, 22, 28, 30, 47, 82x

Fort Mason has something for everyone: performances, festivals, shows, food, museums, classes, the San Francisco African-American Historical and Cultural Society, the Museum of Craft and Folk Art, the Museu ItaloAmericano and even improv comedy, just to name a few. Enjoy a play by day, have a stroll through an art gallery and finish up with a healthy dinner at Greens restaurant. Check the website to see what's new.

66BALMY number 40 map G

ADDRESS 591 guerrero @ 18th street **TELEPHONE** 522-0502 **WEBSITE** www.66balmy.com **OPENING HOURS** thu-fri 2pm-7pm, sat-sun 12pm-5pm **CREDIT CARDS** visa, mastercard, amex **MUNI** 14, 26, 33, 49, j

66balmy gallery showcases artists who have already proven their talent and are now rising stars. "Ascending, not emerging," says owner Jim Serchak. French-born, San Francisco-based Justine Formentelli is one artist being featured. She tours the world and sends her work back as she goes: images from India, Laos, Brazil and Bolivia – it's a beautiful collection. Make sure you check out Balmy Alley (the original home of 66balmy) and its outdoor murals off 24th Street between Treat and Harrison.

The "Roots of Spirit" mural turns a boring wall complete with barred windows into an intriguing scene you'll stop to wonder about. Gain some insight and admiration on a tour with Precita Eyes. You'll get a real feel for the Mission neighborhood as you walk through alleys and back streets that you might not have entered otherwise, seeing murals painted by children, local painters and even world-famous artists.

number 41 map H

PRECITA EYES MURAL TOURS

ADDRESS 2981 24th street @ harrison **TELEPHONE** 285-2287 **WEBSITE** www.precitaeyes.org **OPENING HOURS** visitor center mon-fri 10am-5pm, sat 10am-4pm, sun 12pm-4pm, tour sat-sun 1:30pm check websites for updates **CREDIT CARDS** visa, mastercard **PRICE** tour $12 **MUNI** 12, 27

Grab a seat and enjoy the view of the bay, the city and the 80-foot bottle of Coca-Cola. You'll find tons of places to eat here, from Gilroy Garlic Fries to steaks at Acme Chophouse. Stop at MoMo's (760 2nd street @ king) for a drink on your way in or on your way home. The kids can play their own games behind left field, where there's a miniature stadium. And if you think there's not enough here to keep your attention, remember there's also a baseball game going on.

ADDRESS 24 willie mays plaza **TELEPHONE** 972-2000 **WEBSITE** www.pacbellpark.com **OPENING HOURS** seasonal **CREDIT CARDS** visa, mastercard **PRICE** from $10 **MUNI** 10, 15, 30, 45, 47, 76, n; caltrain; bart: Montgomery, then shuttle

PACBELL PARK number 42 map D

KABUKI SPRINGS & SPA

number 43 map D

ADDRESS 1750 geary @ webster **TELEPHONE** 922-6000 **WEBSITE** www.kabukisprings.com **OPENING HOURS** daily 10am-9:45pm; communal bath hours: women: sun wed fri; men: mon thu sat; coed: tue (clothing required) **CREDIT CARDS** visa, mastercard, amex **PRICE** javanese lulur for 80 minutes $115 **MUNI** 2, 3, 4, 22, 38,

"Javanese Lulur Body Treatment" sounds exotic enough to get you in the door, but then there's talk about "Jasmine Frangipani scented flower oil" and "turmeric and rice skin scrub" and finally "a traditional yogurt application and an exotic flower bath." But enough talk… The experts at Kabuki are now ready to wow your senses and soothe your soul. Book yourself a treatment and leave the world behind.

BODY, MIND & SOUL

You wake up in the morning and have a double-decaf-non-fat-soy-latte for breakfast; then you **hike a trail, ride a bike, rollerblade, hum a mantra** and cleanse your body in a spa. It's lunchtime by now, so you grab a wheatgrass-herb-orange-peel juice with your curried-tofu-bean-sprout sandwich, then soothe your bones with a massage, **climb some rocks**, have some more bean curd and finish off your day with a plastic tube pumping oxygen with a twist of sage up your nose. **Welcome to California**.

San Francisco is an island. Not physically, of course, but practically. Politically, economically, and socially, San Francisco is a place far away from much of the rest of the United States, if not the whole planet. And San Franciscans wouldn't have it any other way. Sure, there are high rents and everything from gasoline to beer costs a fortune, but people operate on a slightly **different wavelength** here.

"If I weren't so addicted to organic foods, I could have extra money for a weekend trip away," a friend says. But that's the way she chooses to live her life and no one here is going to tell her any different. (Well of course, they'll tell her plenty, and she'll listen, but in San Francisco, you're free to do your own thing).

Yoga studios, vegetarian restaurants, **organic juice bars**, Zen centers, natural grocery stores, bell ceremonies, pre-dawn trips to see the sun rise on top of **Mount Tamalpais**, walks on the foggy beach, hikes or bikes in nearby **Marin County** or **Alameda County** – there's a whole other world out here. Eat healthy, live healthy, be healthy – that's the philosophy.

Talk to the woman who blends your **smoothie**. Ask her what fruits are in season and where she lives and why she likes it there. Ask the grocer in the small corner store about the **organic carrots**; he'll probably tell you where they come from, and suggest it would be a fun day trip. Strike up a conversation with **the masseuse** turning your shoulder into Jell-O and she'll happily tell you why she loves San Francisco and why she wouldn't live anywhere else. Talk to anyone and you'll soon learn why **people love it here**.

There are a zillion good-for-you things to do in the city – and new ones pop up all the time. **Ferry Plaza Farmer's Market** recently moved from a parking lot to its new prime location at the **Ferry Building** and is a great place to start off your day (if it's Saturday, Sunday, Tuesday or Thursday). It's a telling sign when a farmer's market gets such prime real estate in a city. The location might have been turned into a department store or some fancy tourist area, but instead it's a beautiful market full of fresh flowers, groceries and fresh air. Pick up some fresh-from-the-garden produce, a bouquet of flowers and just-baked bread and enjoy the view of the bay.

Health food stores are a booming trade in the city. Many have a huge selection of goods for a healthy picnic and wonderful ready-made sandwiches and other yummy goodies.

Whether you're vegan, carnivore, vegetarian or omnivore, your options aren't limited to just picnics in the park. As more proof that health is important in San Francisco, the vegan restaurant **Millennium** moved from its drab Civic Center location to a top spot downtown. It's in a beautiful old building (the Savoy Hotel) with old-world charm – an oddly appropriate place for new-world vegan cuisine. **Greens restaurant**, however, still has one of the best locations of any restaurant in town: Fort Mason.

With people like Lisa Bach (aka Juicey Lucy) quitting the corporate world to open up a local juice bar – and making it work – it's no wonder San Francisco is a haven for the health conscious. Lisa/Lucy slows people down, reminding them to enjoy life and appreciate the health they have and encouraging them to do a little more to improve it.

BODY, MIND & SOUL

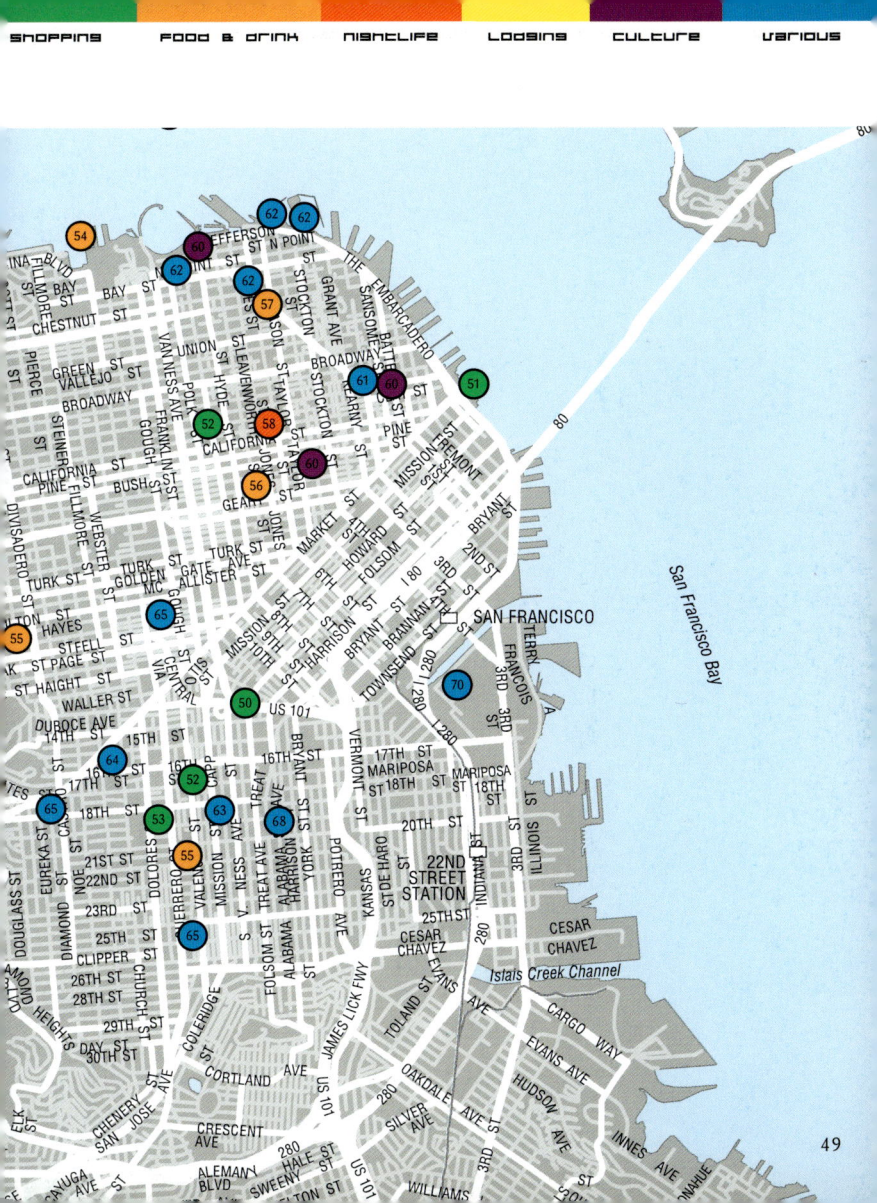

This busy grocery started out in the 1970s as a little storefront on 16th Street run by members of an ashram. It's still independent, collectively run, worker-owned and -operated and fun to browse around. Make sure you check out all the bins of spices, teas, grains, pastas, cereals, trail mixes and who knows what else. There are olives you've never heard of, organic beer, soy margarine and more than five kinds of salt – who knew? Pick up just enough for a picnic or load up for the week.

RAINBOW GROCERY CO-OP number 50 map G

ADDRESS 1745 folsom @ 13th street **TELEPHONE** 863-0620 **WEBSITE** www.rainbowgrocery.org **OPENING HOURS** daily 9am-9pm **CREDIT CARDS** visa, mastercard, amex **MUNI** 9, 12, 14, 22, 27, 33, 47

shopping　　food & drink　　nightlife　　lodging　　culture　　various

FERRY PLAZA FARMER'S MARKET

number 51 map D

ADDRESS ferry building, embarcadero @ market **TELEPHONE** 353-5650 **WEBSITE** www.ferryplazafarmersmarket.com **OPENING HOURS** sat 8am-2pm, tue 10am-2pm, thu 3pm-7pm, sun 9am-3pm (garden market) **CREDIT CARDS** varies **PRICE** free entry **MUNI** 2, 6, 7, 9, 14, 21, 31, 32, 66,71, f, j, k, l, m, n,bart: embarcadero

Grab a fresh baguette from Acme Bread, slice through a few shiny organic tomatoes, gather fresh leaves of baby chard, sip an iced tea from the Imperial Tea Court and you're ready to sit at a table by the bay and enjoy. Stroll through Book Passage, a legendary Bay Area bookstore; if you get stuck in there for hours and get hungry, there's always good food and a view at The Slanted Door. Or just stroll around some more and pick out a sweet apricot or a fancy pastry for dessert. Choose a bouquet of bright flowers for your hotel room and your morning has blossomed into a great day.

If a friend blindfolded you and brought you into this store, when you opened your eyes you'd almost certainly say, "Ooh!" It might be an Ooh of shock and disgust or one of pleasure and titillation – or maybe a little of both. Joani Blank founded the store in 1977 and has been providing "accurate sex information and quality sex toys" ever since. The store has a whole section dedicated to waterproof "Bath Buddies", such as "I Rub My Duckie" and "Waves of Pleasure". Browse the shelves a while, you'll be surprised what's available. Ooh!

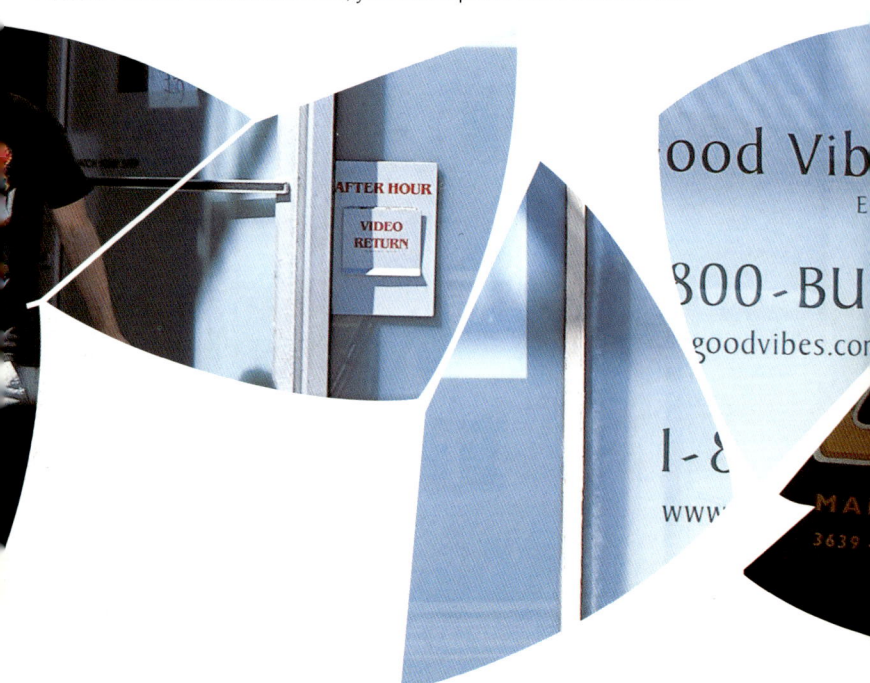

GOOD VIBRATIONS number 52 map C, D

ADDRESS two locations (1) 603 valencia @ 17th street (2) 1620 polk @ sacramento **TELEPHONE** 522-5460, 345-0400 **WEBSITE** www.goodvibes.com **OPENING HOURS** (1) sun-wed 11am-7pm, thu-sat 11am-8pm, (2) sun-thu 11am-7pm, fri-sat 11am-9pm **CREDIT CARDS** visa, mastercard **MUNI** (1) 14, 26, 49, j, bart: 16th & mission (2) 1, 19, 27, 47, 49, california cable car

number 53 map G **BI-RITE**

ADDRESS 3639 18th street @ guerrero **TELEPHONE** 241-9760 **OPENING HOURS** mon-fri 10am-9pm, sat 9am-8pm, sun 9am-8pm **CREDIT CARDS** visa, mastercard, amex **PRICE** sandwiches $6 **MUNI** 14, 26, 33, 49, j

Just down the street from Dolores Park, Bi-Rite is a local grocery store that will make you want to move into the neighborhood. Stock up on picnic supplies at the superb deli counter and put all your fillings into one of the fresh breads. This is not going to be an average picnic, not with spicy Niman Ranch meatloaf sandwiches, pine nut and herb brie, fresh olives and salsas and Ciao Bella gelato.

Established by the Zen Center in 1979, Greens has never stopped being busy. With 30-foot ceilings, a sweeping view of the Golden Gate Bridge and the harbor, and food tasty enough to convert any carnivore, your only dilemma will be figuring out when you can come back again. Never fear, with executive chef Annie Somerville's cookbook, "Everyday Greens", you can recreate the scene, flavors and experience of Greens when you get home.

GREENS number 54 map B, C

ADDRESS fort mason building, laguna @ marina **TELEPHONE** 771-6222 **WEBSITE** www.greensrestaurant.com
OPENING HOURS tue-sat 12pm-2:30pm, mon-sat 5:30pm-9pm, sun 10:30am-2pm **CREDIT CARDS** visa, mastercard, amex **PRICE** $17 **MUNI** 10, 28, 49

number 55 map G # HERBIVORE

ADDRESS two locations (1) 983 valencia @ 21st street (2) 531 divisadero @ fell **TELEPHONE** 826-5657, 885-7133 **OPENING HOURS** sun-thu 11am-10pm, fri-sat 11am-11pm **CREDIT CARDS** visa, mastercard **PRICE** $8 **MUNI** (1) 14, 26, 49, bart: 24th & mission (2) 6, 7, 21, 24

Even carnivores will confess that the vegetarian "shawarma wrap" isn't lacking a thing – not even meat. Try the charbroiled veggies with red peppers, tomatoes, and shitake mushrooms. Sip an organically farmed merlot or Belgian ale and if the weather's right, head to the cozy back patio. The Divisadero location also serves brunch on weekends.

Housed in the century-old Hotel Savoy, Millennium is 100% vegan, 100% organic and 100% 21st century. Have a blackberry "mojito" (the cocktails are organic too!) while you're waiting for your "seitan marsala" with gravy and mashed potatoes (a popular dish). Afterwards, refresh your spirits with a "restorative cocktail," such as the non-alcoholic Health Tonic. Keep an eye out for specially themed evenings, when there's only one thing on the menu. Recently, it was the Flaming Hot Chili Dinner.

MILLENNIUM number 56 map D

ADDRESS 580 geary @ jones **TELEPHONE** 345-3900 **WEBSITE** www.millenniumrestaurant.com **OPENING HOURS** daily 5:30pm-9:30pm **CREDIT CARDS** visa, mastercard, amex **PRICE** $17 **MUNI** 2, 3, 4, 27, 38, f, j, k, l, m, n, bart: powell st

JUICEY LUCY'S

number 57 map D

ADDRESS 703 columbus @ filbert **TELEPHONE** 786-1285 **WEBSITE** www.juiceylucy.com **OPENING HOURS** daily 11am-6pm **CREDIT CARDS** none **PRICE** $5 **MUNI** 15, 30, 41, powell/mason cable car

"Do you have three minutes?" Juicey Lucy asks. She would rather have you sit and relax for a few minutes than place an order to go – she doesn't even have to-go cups. Try a Vegetable Vitality smoothie with seasonal roots, veggies, ginger and garlic, or maybe an Ambrosia juice – fruit of the gods. The Sesame Tamari Baked Tofu Sandwich is hearty enough to get you through the rest of the day – and what a day it will be. "Drink well, feel well, live well," Lucy says. And take your time.

GRACE AFTER HOURS number 58 map D

ADDRESS 1100 california @ taylor **TELEPHONE** 749-6358 **WEBSITE** www.gracecathedral.org **OPENING HOURS** second friday of every month, 6pm-9pm **PRICE** free, donations welcome **MUNI** 1, 27

You feel like you could be in a small town in Europe rather than in the center of San Francisco: a church lights up with candles, harp music floats through the evening air, hand bells ring softly and people are at peace with the world. On the second Friday of every month, people join together on top of Nob Hill at the majestic Grace Cathedral to walk through two labyrinths. The indoor labyrinth is a beautiful wool tapestry, while the outdoor one is terrazzo stone. Forget therapy, prescription drugs and counseling … try walking these paths first.

Stay right next to Golden Gate Park and wake up to a jog, a bike ride or a pleasant walk through the vast greenery of the park. A 1905 Victorian building, Stanyan Park Hotel has 36 rooms and suites – the larger ones with kitchens – where you'll feel as though you're a guest in a Victorian residence. You're also steps away from Haight Street and all of its shops, restaurants, and wackiness.

number 59 map F # STANYAN PARK HOTEL

ADDRESS 750 stanyan @ waller **TELEPHONE** 751-1000 **WEBSITE** www.stanyanpark.com **CREDIT CARDS** visa, mastercard, amex **PRICE** from $130 **MUNI** 6, 7, 33, 43, 66, 71, n

shopping   food & drink   nightlife   lodging   culture   various

There are at least three great spots in town where you can forget your worries and laugh as hard and as loud as you like. (1) Comedy on the Square has consistently good talent coming in and out of their Union Square theater – keep an eye on their seasonal schedule. (2) Cobb's Comedy Club is housed in the beautiful old brick cannery building near Ghirardelli Square. (3) Punchline Comedy Club has been getting hoots for over 20 years.

number 60 map C, D
LAUGHTER: THE BEST MEDICINE
ADDRESS three locations (1) 533 sutter @ powell (2) 2801 leavenworth @ beach (3) 444 battery @ washington **TELEPHONE** (1) 522-8900 (2) 928-4320 (3) 397-7573 **WEBSITE** (1) www.comedyonthesquare.com (2) www.cobbscomedyclub.com (3) www.punchlinecomedyclub.com **OPENING HOURS** check websites **CREDIT CARDS** visa, mastercard **PRICE** from $5 for special nights, often two-drink minimum **MUNI** (1) 2, 3, 4, 38, 30, 45 powell/mason & powell/hyde cable cars (2) 30, 32, powell/hyde cable car (3) 1, 12

ADDRESS 750 kearny @ washington **TELEPHONE** 399-9700 **WEBSITE** www.truspa.com **OPENING HOURS** mon, tue, thu, fri 9am-8pm, wed 12pm-8pm, sat 10am-8pm, sun 11am-6pm **CREDIT CARDS** visa, mastercard, amex **PRICE** 65 minutes $145 **MUNI** 9, 15

number 61 map D # TRŪ

With names like "Sugar Daddy," "Jungle Love," and "Vanilla Sky," it's not immediately clear whether this is a shop of confections, libations or stimulations. Actually, it's all three – it's a spa. Head into the Tropical Rainforest Room, complete with jungle sounds and skimpy loincloth-towels, and all of your senses will be soothed and smoothed away using natural materials, from coconut and kukui nut to papaya and mango. Finally, you'll be rinsed off under a warm rain forest shower.

BLAZING SADDLES number 62 map D

ADDRESS four locations (1) 1095 columbus @ Francisco (2) 2715 hyde @ north point (3) pier 41 (4) pier 43 **TELEPHONE** 202-8888 **WEBSITE** www.blazingsaddles.com **OPENING HOURS** daily 8am-8pm (late night returns possible) **CREDIT CARDS** visa, mastercard, amex **PRICE** from $28/day **MUNI** (1) 30 powell/mason cable car (2) 30 powell/hyde cable car (3) 32, f (4) 32, 4

A favorite local outing is to ride a bicycle over Golden Gate Bridge to Sausalito and Tiburon, enjoy the views, have lunch, then relax and jump on the ferry back to San Francisco. You beat traffic, get some exercise and see the city and its views in a way a car cannot. Blazing Saddles provides maps with bike-friendly routes highlighted through the Presidio and Golden Gate Park and Marin County. Of course you don't have to follow the map – this is freedom, baby!

Don't worry if you hear someone order a tall glass of oxygen with a splash of lavender. This is California after all, and in the land of environmental everything, you can be served oxygen in a small tube through your nose with a hint of whatever herb you'd like to have spice up your life (lavender, ginseng, ylang-ylang, sage, sandalwood, etc.). Wash it down with your favorite herbal elixir — try the "Mental Eclipse." Or stick with what you know: sushi and sake. There are no guarantees, but you can be pretty certain this is better than sitting in traffic.

ADDRESS 795 valencia @ 19th street **TELEPHONE** 255-2102 **WEBSITE** www.2202bar.com **OPENING HOURS** tue-thu & sun 6pm-midnight, fri-sat 6pm-2am **CREDIT CARDS** visa, mastercard **PRICE** ten minutes for $10 **MUNI** 14, 26, 49, j

number 63 map G **2202 OXYGEN BAR**

NICKEL SPA number 64 map G

ADDRESS 2187 market @ sanchez **TELEPHONE** 756-1765 **WEBSITE** www.nickelspa.com **OPENING HOURS** tue-fri 11am-9pm, sat 10am-9pm, sun-mon 1pm-9pm **CREDIT CARDS** visa, mastercard **PRICE** 60-minute facial $80 **MUNI** 37, f, j, k, l, m

There's no time here to mess around with fancy names that don't mean anything. At Nickel Spa, they get right to the point. You just know the "Morning After Rescue Gel" is going to revitalize your skin after a tough night out on the town. From Paris to New York and now San Francisco, founder Philippe Dumont knows that men want results fast, so his products have more active ingredients and larger sized tubes. Gift certificates are available for men who need a push from their partner. Of course, not everything here is macho… the name is pronounced "nee-kel."

Want to recuperate after a day and night on the town? Hatha, Iyengar or Soul Flow might be just what the herbalist ordered. Over the years, Yoga Tree has turned into a small 'chain' of studios in the city, and enjoys huge popularity amongst locals looking for relaxation and rejuvenation of mind, body and spirit. Classes are offered daily from about 7:00am to 7:00pm for beginners and advanced practitioners alike. They also offer massages (at $70/hour) and a retail store. Pick up a mat and start your day in this spiritual city with a sun salutation!

number 65 map F, G **YOGA TREE**

ADDRESS four locations (1) 1234 valencia @ 23rd street (2) 519 hayes @ octavia (3) 780 stanyan @ waller (4) 97 collingwood @ 18th street **TELEPHONE** 647-9707 **WEBSITE** www.yogatreesf.com **OPENING HOURS** 7am-7pm **CREDIT CARDS** visa, mastercard, amex **PRICE** drop-in $12 **MUNI** 26, 14, 49, bart: 24th & mission

SKATING IN THE PARK number 66 map E

ADDRESS 6th avenue @ fulton **TELEPHONE** 752-1967 **WEBSITE** www.cora.org **OPENING HOURS** sun and some holidays **PRICE** from $6 per hour **MUNI** 5, 21, 31

On Sundays, parts of Golden Gate Park close down to vehicular traffic and open up to thousands of skaters. This a great place to learn to skate or improve your skills while dancing to music. Meet near 6th avenue @ fulton. Rent skates at the following shops around the park: Skate Pro (27th avenue @ irving); Skate Shop (fulton @ 7th avenue); skates on haight (1818 haight @ stanyan).

shopping   food & drink   nightlife   lodging   culture   various

Most tourists don't get beyond Alcatraz, the famed island prison, but another stop on the Blue & Gold Ferry will bring you to miles of hiking and biking trails, picnic tables, beaches and – best of all – surprising surprising solitude. This is an ideal, quick get-away-from-it-all spot, without really going very far away. You can camp overnight (call first for reservations), rent kayaks and bicycles or just stroll around the trails. There isn't much in terms of food, so plan a picnic – Molinari's is a good bet. Keep an eye on the ferry schedule though, because if you miss the last one, you'll be spending the night even if you hadn't planned on it!

number 67 map C **ANGEL ISLAND**

ADDRESS angel island, take blue & gold ferry from pier 41 **TELEPHONE** 394-0500 **WEBSITE** www.angelisland.com **OPENING HOURS** seasonal **CREDIT CARDS** visa, mastercard, amex **PRICE** round-trip $12 **MUNI** 32, f

ADDRESS 2295 harrison @ 19th street **TELEPHONE** 550-0515 **WEBSITE** www.touchstoneclimbing.com
OPENING HOURS mon-fri 6:30am-10pm, sat-sun 10am-6pm **CREDIT CARDS** visa, mastercard, amex **PRICE** $18 non-member day pass **MUNI** 12

MISSION CLIFFS number 68 map H

Had enough of museums and sushi bars? Climb the walls in this former warehouse and burn off that coconut curry you had for lunch. This is a full-featured indoor climbing space with lead-climbs and top-roping for all categories of climbers. For those not used to hanging from rocks by your fingernails, lessons are available and there is also a full gym and sauna. With 14,000 square feet of climbing terrain, you're bound to find a wall to climb.

Monterey pines and eucalyptus trees surround you, sometimes so densely that it's difficult to believe there is a metropolitan city just a stone's throw away. The military turned this area over to the National Park Service in 1995 and the course was then opened to the public. After your game, wander over to Inspiration Point for a stunning view of the bay and Alcatraz. Warning: if the fog sets in, it adds a whole new dimension to your game.

number 69 map A **PRESIDIO GOLF COURSE**

ADDRESS 300 finley @ pacific **TELEPHONE** 561-4653 **WEBSITE** www.presidiogolf.com **OPENING HOURS** daily **CREDIT CARDS** visa, mastercard **PRICE** mon-thu $42 **MUNI** 29

Mission Bay Golf Center has two tiers and 66 tees just outside of downtown, plus views of the city skyline and PacBell Park. Have lunch at Stix Roadhouse Café, and improve your swing without even leaving town. It can be hard to find, so just keep looking for the nets draped between the triple-tall-telephone-poles. Half-hour golf lessons for $50 are also available.

MISSION BAY GOLF CENTER number 70 map H

ADDRESS 1200 6th street @ channel **TELEPHONE** 431-7888 **WEBSITE** www.missionbaygolfclub.com **OPENING HOURS** mon 11:30am-10pm, tue-sun 7am-10pm **CREDIT CARDS** visa, mastercard **PRICE** seventy balls for $8 **MUNI** 10, 15, 19, 30, 45, 47, 76, plus a short walk

notes

shopping   food & drink   nightlife   lodging   culture   various

SOPHISTICATE

shopping　　　　food & drink　　　　nightlife　　　　lodging　　　　culture　　　　various

Any San Franciscan will tell you their city is the cultural center of the west coast. From murals in the **Mission** to galleries in **SoMa**, poetry slams to author signings, one-man stage shows to the latest modern art gallery opening (complete with cocktails) the city is a **theater for the senses**.

The fashion and art of the various neighborhoods are as distinct as the neighborhoods themselves, although things tend to get mixed up in San Francisco. Haight-Ashbury hippies show up at **trendy SoMa galleries**, while businessmen dump their ties and wingtips to loosen up in a **Valencia Corridor** art gallery. Choose from the grunge of some of the Mission and SoMa art studios or the more commercial galleries on Geary Street or in Union Square.

A good place to start is in the heart of the tourist district: Union Square. There's a large kiosk on the west side of the square called TIX that sells half-price tickets to concerts, theater, ballet, comedy, musicals, dance performances and whatever else may be going on in town. Stand right in front of the window and plan your day around **what's playing**, **where** and **when**.

You might get great seats for a small production by a company running their first show or a Broadway hit that's just come to San Francisco. Or you could just hang out in a bar near a **gallery** or **theater** and watch the "art" there for a while. Sip wine with the best of them and talk about the latest show, gallery or vineyard. Even if you're not an expert, you can at least look like you know what you're talking about – or talk like you know what you're looking at.

There are many excellent theaters just west of Union Square, but if you're in the Valencia Corridor, check out a small theater called The Marsh. It features smaller productions, and it's the kind of place where, later on, people recognize someone on screen or on stage and say, "Hey, I saw that guy at **The Marsh**." It's one example of a smaller theater in town where you might be sitting so close to the stage you have to move your feet when the actors walk by!

San Francisco is one of those cities – like Paris, New York or Prague – where walking aimlessly around can be the best way to see the place. Stroll away from Union Square and admire the **attention to detail** put into the buildings constructed after the 1906 earthquake. Go west of Van Ness for a look at some beauties of architecture – San Francisco's pre-earthquake Victorians and Edwardians. Many of these have been kept in pristine condition inside and out, and one of the most elaborate (and public) examples is the **Haas-Lilienthal House**. Get an inside look at how San Francisco's rich and famous lived over a century ago.

Other architectural gems are in harder-to-find places, or else in spots where you wouldn't necessarily look. Some of the older buildings in the Financial District have extremely grandiose lobbies, for example. Splurge and have brunch at the **Palace Hotel**, one of the most famous hotels in the world. Sit in the **Garden Court** and it won't be hard to think of the city's elite having the same brunch 100 years ago. Try to catch a film at the **Castro Theater**. You might not remember what you saw there, but you'll remember where you saw it – the architecture is superb. Keep your eyes open, as history oozes out of the cracks in this city.

Weekly email newsletters like sfstation.com are an excellent source of what's going on. They are long and packed with events and information. If you've never been to a **poetry slam**, then you're in the right place. Or you might find out about a gallery opening right near your hotel.

SOPHISTICATE

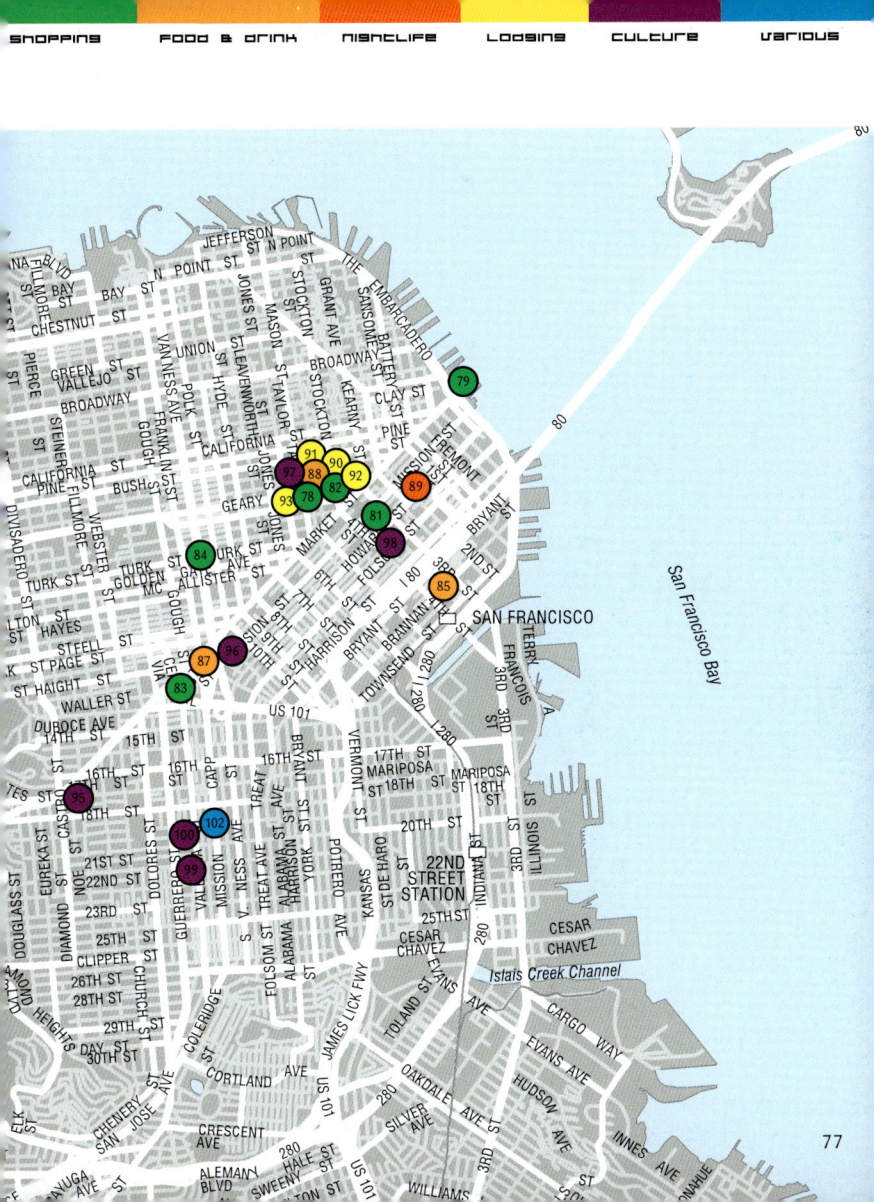

URBAN OUTFITTERS number 78 map D

ADDRESS 80 powell @ ellis **TELEPHONE** 989-1515 **WEBSITE** www.urbanoutfitters.com **OPENING HOURS** mon-sat 9:30am-9:30pm, sun 10:30am-9pm **CREDIT CARDS** visa, mastercard, amex **MUNI** 2, 3, 4, 30, f, j, k, l, m, n, bart: powell st.

True to its name, this place has anything and everything for the city dweller. Where else will you find a welcome mat that reads "Rental Sweet Rental"? You'll also get trendy men's and women's clothing, useful but frivolous housewares (goldfish-printed plastic shower curtains), candles and even furniture. The shop itself is a raw warehouse: four floors of exposed water pipes and air vents, brick everywhere and product lines with names like Porn Star, Rocket Dog and Free People.

One of the bay area's liveliest bookstores has now come to the Ferry Building. Known for its many courses and workshops for writers, Book Passage is a great place to hear writers reading from their work. Browse the aisles for something to sit down outside with. Then pick up a sandwich or some fresh fruit from the market outside, find a quiet spot and lose yourself between the pages.

ADDRESS ferry building, embarcadero @ market **TELEPHONE** 835-1020 **WEBSITE** www.bookpassage.com
OPENING HOURS mon-fri 10am-5pm, sat 9 am-6pm, sun 11am-5pm **CREDIT CARDS** visa, mastercard, amex
MUNI 2, 6, 7, 9, 14, 21, 31, 32, 66, 71, f, j, k, l, m, n, bart: embarcadero

number 79 map D **BOOK PASSAGE**

WISHBONE number 80 map E

ADDRESS 601 irving @ 7th street **TELEPHONE** 252-8511 **WEBSITE** www.wishbonesf.com **OPENING HOURS** daily 11:30am-7pm **CREDIT CARDS** visa, mastercard **MUNI** 6, 43, 44, 66, 71, n

This is a store with a sense of humor. It's full of generic calendars, greeting cards and scented candles, but there are other gems like princess phones, books of Mad Libs and sushi print pajamas. Take your pick from the array of Paul Frank products – you know, the ones with that saucy little monkey. They've got dog leashes and collars, pajamas, bathrobes, watches, clocks and handbags. If nothing else, at least get yourself a "Hello Pitbull" T-shirt. Meow.

The store at the Museum of Modern Art is a treasure chest of books, toys, posters and art. Every item seems like an invention. "What does that thing do?" you'll wonder, and then you'll pick it up and try to figure it out. The store carries beautiful glasswork, designs you've never seen before and quite a selection of kids' games and books. If you see something you like, grab it, because you're not likely to find it elsewhere. Once you're done shopping, don't forget to visit the museum!

number 81 map D SFMOMA MUSEUMSTORE

ADDRESS two locations (1) 151 3rd street @ mission (2) sf international airport (pre-security, in the international terminal main hall) **TELEPHONE** 357-4035 **WEBSITE** www.sfmoma.org **OPENING HOURS** (1) daily mon-wed, fri-sun 10am-6:30pm, thu 10am-9:30pm (2) daily 9am-6pm **CREDIT CARDS** visa, mastercard, amex **MUNI** 6, 7, 9, 12, 14, 15, 21, 30, 38, 45, f, j, k, l, m, n, bart: montgomery st, powell st (2) bart: sfo (airport)

Housewares, kitchenware, clothing for anywhere, shoes, jewelry, and beauty products all arranged tastefully in this urban San Francisco warehouse-turned-French-country-home. What keeps the clientele coming back is the unique line of products not found in other shops. At the same time, you'll find names such as Michael Stars and Nanette Lepore. One woman said she felt so comfortable in the shop that she could live there.

ANTHROPOLOGIE number 82 map D

ADDRESS 880 market @ powell **TELEPHONE** 434-2210 **WEBSITE** www.anthropologie.com **OPENING HOURS** mon-sat 10am-8pm, sun 11am-7pm **CREDIT CARDS** visa, mastercard, amex **MUNI** 6, 7, 9, 14, 21, 30, 45, f, j, k, l, m, n, bart: powell st

number 83 map G # FLAX ART & DESIGN

ADDRESS 1699 market @ valencia **TELEPHONE** 552-2355 **WEBSITE** www.flaxart.com **OPENING HOURS** mon-sat 9:30am-6pm, sun 11am-5pm **CREDIT CARDS** visa, mastercard, amex **MUNI** 6, 7, 26, f

Although officially an art supply store, this is really a store about inspiration. You won't just find glue and paint here; there are journals and stationery, hundreds of pens, gift boxes, photo albums in wood or leather, unique CD cases, toasters, teapots, calendars and candles … it's a huge warehouse of a space. Make sure you check out the collection of paper. It might not sound exciting, but when you see the variety, your imagination is bound to start flowing. In fact, this happens quite a bit while you walk around FLAX.

Have a seat, relax and listen to the inside scoop straight from the writer. ACWLPB has readings or other book-related events practically every night. Come hear what the writer has to say about his or her book before the movie comes out – sometimes even before the book comes out. Readings are usually in the evenings, so afterwards head over to nearby Hayes Street for dinner.

A CLEAN WELL-LIGHTED PLACE FOR BOOKS number 84 map C

ADDRESS 601 van ness @ turk **TELEPHONE** 441-6670 **WEBSITE** www.bookstore.com **OPENING HOURS** mon-sat 10am-11pm, sun 10am-9pm **CREDIT CARDS** visa, mastercard, amex **MUNI** 21, 31, 38, 47, 49

number 85 map D **BACAR**

ADDRESS 448 brannan @ 3rd street **TELEPHONE** 904-4100 **WEBSITE** www.bacarsf.com **OPENING HOURS** mon-thu 5:30pm-midnight, fri-sat 5:30pm-1am, sun 5:30pm-11pm **CREDIT CARDS** visa, mastercard, amex **PRICE** $23 **MUNI** 15, 30, 45

In the heyday of the dot-com boom, this place was really happening. A few years later, it's still around – which is more than you can say for many of the local restaurants in SoMa. Bright and airy with lots of white and brick, Bacar is more than eye candy. Try sumptuous entrees such as mesquite grilled Angus rib eye steak and kennebec fries, or oven-roasted, sumac-marinated Colorado lamb sirloin. The herbed spaetzle and apricot appetizer is worth a taste, and so is the wine.

Bright and airy, healthy and sunny, this place makes you want to become an artist – or at least sit next to one while you sip your double Chai latte. A combined art gallery and café, you're welcome to lounge for a while and gaze to your heart's content. Get a hot coffee and stick around for one of the many evening events, or grab a tea and walk slowly around the gallery, nodding your head a lot.

ADDRESS 1200 9th avenue @ lincoln **TELEPHONE** 504-0060 **WEBSITE** www.thecanvasgallery.com **OPENING HOURS** sun-wed 8am-12am, thu-sat 8am-2am **CREDIT CARDS** visa, mastercard **PRICE** $7 **MUNI** 6, 43, 44, n

CANVAS number 86 map E

ADDRESS 45 rose @ market **TELEPHONE** 703-0403 **WEBSITE** www.hotelbiron.com **OPENING HOURS** tue-sun 11am-2am **CREDIT CARDS** visa, mastercard, amex **PRICE** $6 **MUNI** 6, 7, f

number 87 map G # HOTEL BIRON

Hidden away behind the bustle of Market Street and around the corner from the much easier to find Zuni Café, this little cave of a wine bar is worth the search. Inside, the brick walls make the place as cozy as a wine cellar and create a backdrop for the work of new artists that's a stark contrast from a whitewashed, overly lit museum. As you sip wine and munch on delectable cheeses and fine caviar, you'll lose track of time. The first Thursday of every month there is a reception for a new artist. You can stay for wine and hors d'oeuvres, but not overnight … it's not actually a hotel.

GRAND CAFÉ number 88 map C

ADDRESS 501 geary @ taylor **TELEPHONE** 292-0101 **WEBSITE** www.grandcafe.net **OPENING HOURS** mon-fri 7am-10pm, sat 8am-10pm, sun 9am-10pm **CREDIT CARDS** visa, mastercard, amex **PRICE** café $9, restaurant $21 **MUNI** 2, 3, 4, 27, 38, f, j, k, l, m, n, bart: powell st

You'll think you're in Paris at the turn of the 20th century when you step into the Grand Café. Large oval windows, dark and hard woods and swooping art-deco lines make this corner restaurant a great place to stay a while. The bar just invites you to sit at it – as many do after a nearby theater show. There's a café in front and a dining room in the back. If you only eat in the café at least go have a look at the dining room. Need to stay a while longer? Check out the art deco Hotel Monaco (from $229).

An art gallery with a full liquor license, 111 Minna takes its art – and its bar – seriously. A premiere pop culture gallery, it doubles as a bar, a nightclub and a venue for the literati and glitterati to hang out and hang their work. Saturday nights usually feature DJ Qoöl, but keep an eye on the website to stay up-to-date.

number 89 map D **111 MINNA**

ADDRESS 111 minna @ 2nd street **TELEPHONE** 974-1719 **WEBSITE** www.111minnagallery.com **OPENING HOURS** tue-sat 12pm-8pm, later for parties and events **CREDIT CARDS** none **PRICE** $6 **MUNI** 6, 7, 9, 12, 14, 15, 21, f, j, k, l, m, n, bart: montgomery st

HOTEL TRITON number 90 map D

ADDRESS 324 grant @ bush **TELEPHONE** 394-0500 **WEBSITE** www.hoteltriton.com **CREDIT CARDS** visa, mastercard, amex **PRICE** $150 **MUNI** 2, 3, 4, 30, 45, f, j, k, l, m, n, bart: powell st

Stars and moons, blues and golds, odd shapes and fuzzy furniture ... you might think you have fallen down the hole with Alice in Wonderland. But this is no mere child's play: there are fireside wine and beer parties in the mezzanine art gallery, celebrity suites designed by the late Jerry Garcia, 100% down comforters in every room and Mr. Bubble and rubber duckies in every bathtub.

Ruby-red floors, dark wood-covered walls, plush seating … you'll just melt into the scenery when the music begins. San Francisco Performances has a regular concert series in the Salon downstairs and the hotel plays host to a number of other cultural events, from music to literature. Have a drink at the full bar in the lobby or dinner next door at the French bistro, Café Andrée. The rooms are very tastefully decorated, but with all there is to do just in the lobby, when will you have time to spend in the room?

number 91 map D **HOTEL REX**

ADDRESS 562 sutter @ powell **TELEPHONE** 433-4434 **WEBSITE** www.thehotelrex.com **CREDIT CARDS** visa, mastercard, amex **PRICE** from $225 **MUNI** 2, 3, 4, 30, 45, f, j, k, l, m, n, bart: powell st.

Literature reigns supreme in this 1906 inn renovated to suggest Thomas Jefferson's Monticello retreat in Virginia. From the white pillars to the chandeliers, it's the essence of colonial America. But this is not a stodgy inn filled with old men in wigs. The hottest in San Francisco literati come to read from their latest masterpiece every Wednesday at 5:30 in the library. Hipper still, on the first Wednesday of every month there's a meeting of the "Wild Writing Women." Each room has a speed dial to a nearby Borders bookstore, and a bellman will pick up your purchase for you.

MONTICELLO INN number 92 map D

ADDRESS 127 ellis @ mason **TELEPHONE** 394-0661 **WEBSITE** www.monticelloinn.com **CREDIT CARDS** visa, mastercard, amex **PRICE** from $219 **MUNI** 2, 3, 4, 30, 38, f, j, k, l, m, n, bart: powell st.

number 93 map C **CLIFT**

ADDRESS 495 geary @ taylor **TELEPHONE** 775-4700 **WEBSITE** www.clifthotel.com **CREDIT CARDS** visa, mastercard, amex **PRICE** from $325 **MUNI** 2, 3, 4, 27, 38, f, j, k, l, m, n, bart: powell st

Designer Phillippe Starck fused luscious red leather, dark woods, lighted glass and delicately soft lighting to turn the Clift into a hotel where traditional elegance meets present-day glamour. The bar is a cascade of colored glass and a mix of shiny silvers and deep yellows – yet somehow it doesn't clash. In fact, it melts together just as you melt into the scenery. Even if you don't have a drink at the bar, a meal at the restaurant or a snooze in the hotel, at the very least go have a look.

These tours are given by locals who usually live in the neighborhood they're guiding you through. They've studied the history, are passionate about where they live and often know owners both past and present (if you're lucky, they might be able to get you inside a majestic Victorian). City Guides has over 200 volunteers who do such a good job you'll be asking for housing prices by the end of the day.

CITY GUIDES number 94

ADDRESS all over town **TELEPHONE** 557-4266 **WEBSITE** www.sfcityguides.org
OPENING HOURS check schedule, extra tours in spring and fall **PRICE** free, donations welcome

ADDRESS 429 castro @ market **TELEPHONE** 621-6120 **WEBSITE** www.thecastrotheatre.com **OPENING HOURS** check calendar **CREDIT CARDS** none **PRICE** from $8 **MUNI** 24, 35, f, k, l, m

number 95 map G # CASTRO THEATRE

Like at restaurants at the top of skyscrapers, where the food isn't the main attraction, going to the Castro Theatre isn't really about what film is playing. Built in 1922 in Spanish renaissance style, each film begins with a live performance on the theatre's organ, setting the mood and sending you back to an era well before home video. Unlike the mediocre food at those rotating restaurants, here you are bound to enjoy the classic film, too.

Gallery director Charles Linder explains that Linc features, "real art, compared with Fisherman's Wharf art." Although, he admits, "that probably sells better." Linder wanted the space to look like a home and must have succeeded, as visitors often ask if he lives there. Local artists predominate, but the gallery also does exchanges with international artists to help promote them in their home country.

LINC number 96 map G

ADDRESS 1632c market @ rose **TELEPHONE** 503-1981 **WEBSITE** www.lincart.com **OPENING HOURS** tue-sat 12pm-6pm **CREDIT CARDS** visa, mastercard, amex **MUNI** 6,7, f

number 97 map D **TIX**

ADDRESS union square @ powell **TELEPHONE** 433-7827 **WEBSITE** www.theatrebayarea.org/tix **OPENING HOURS** tue-thu 11am-6pm, fri-sat 11am-7pm, sun 11am-3pm **CREDIT CARDS** none **PRICE** half **MUNI** 2, 3, 4, 30, 35, 38, 45, f, j, k, l, m, n, bart: powell st

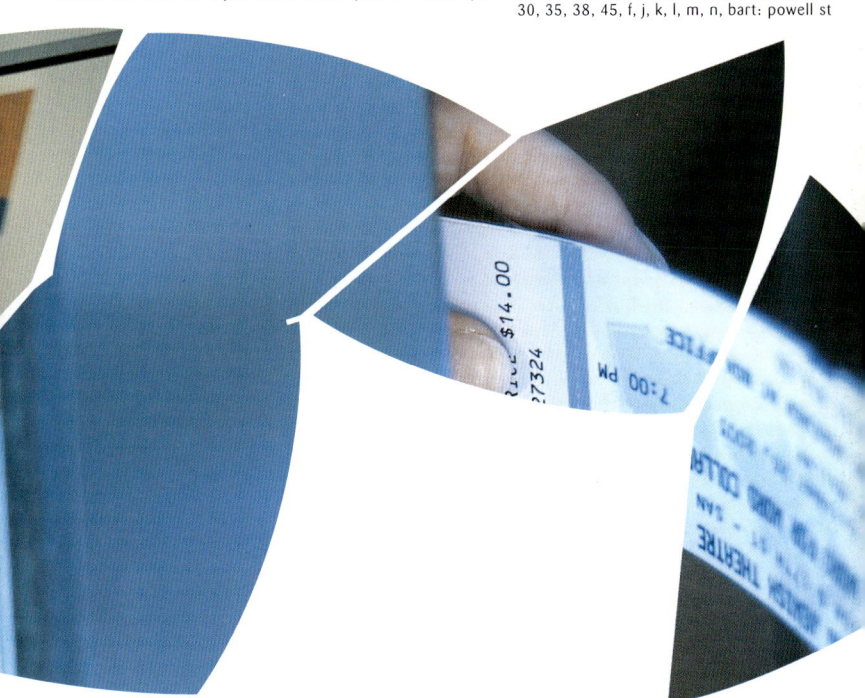

TIX Bay Area is an unsuspecting powerhouse directly on Union Square. On the day of a show, you can get half-price tickets for minor and major performances and events in town: theater, dance, musicals, etc. Walk up and have a look at the board of what's on and your plans for the evening might change before your eyes — many times over. The staff behind the glass can't officially tell you what's good and what's not, so ask others standing around. Many are locals who go to TIX before planning the rest of their day.

YERBA BUENA CENTER FOR THE ARTS number 98 map D

ADDRESS 701 mission @ 3rd street **TELEPHONE** 978-2787 **WEBSITE** www.yerbabuenaarts.org **OPENING HOURS** gallery tue-sun 11am-6pm, theater check schedule **CREDIT CARDS** visa, mastercard **PRICE** gallery $7 **MUNI** 6, 7, 9, 12, 14, 15, 21, 30, 38, 45, f, j, k, l, m, n, bart: montgomery st, powell st

Film, dance, music, lectures, art and theater mean there's pretty much always something buzzing here. From Alonzo King's LINES dance company to a cozy showing of The Velveteen Rabbit at Christmas, you'll get a balanced diet of culture here. Check the schedule for opening night bashes and happy hours. In the summer, enjoy free jazz concerts in the Yerba Buena gardens, just outside the door.

True to their "breeding ground" tagline, The Marsh is a place that grows on you. Many people who come as innocent audience members return again and again, eventually becoming more involved, enrolling in a workshop, coming to a sing-along night or joining the internship program. Monday Night Marsh is a chance to see works in progress by local writers, playwrights, or actors. The place has the feel of an underground club — and you can be a part of it.

number 99 map G **THE MARSH**

ADDRESS 1062 valencia @ 22nd street **TELEPHONE** 641-0235 **WEBSITE** www.themarsh.org **OPENING HOURS** check website **CREDIT CARDS** visa, mastercard **PRICE** varies, from $12 **MUNI** 14, 26, 49, bart: 24th & mission

Artist owned and operated since 1998, City Art is truly for the people, by the people. Local artists display their work and do double-time behind the reception desk. They like to call it "accessible art", meaning it's both unassuming and affordable. But that's about the only theme here. Otherwise, it's a wide range of media: sculpture, oil paintings, etchings, lithography, photography or any combination thereof. You're invited to a free opening show party on the first Friday of each month.

CITY ART number 100 map G

ADDRESS 828 valencia @ 19th street **TELEPHONE** 970-9900 **WEBSITE** www.cityartgallery.org **OPENING HOURS** wed-sun 12pm-9pm **CREDIT CARDS** visa, mastercard **MUNI** 14, 26, 49, bart: 24th & mission

ADDRESS check sunday newspaper or online for weekly listings **WEBSITE** www.sfgate.com/homes
OPENING HOURS sun 1pm-4pm

number 101 # OPEN HOUSES

"Two-bedroom Victorian, hardwood floors, remodeled kitchen, fireplace, garden, parking, view of Golden Gate Bridge." Check out what it's like to live in the city by peeking into the lives of some of its citizens. See what hipsters do to decorate their homes, or check out new loft spaces in SoMa, a mansion in Pacific Heights or a turn-of-the-century Victorian near Golden Gate Park. Bring your imagination and checkbook (or wheelbarrows of cash).

Sean Kelly swooped in on lower rent prices where only a few years ago art studios, galleries and artists were getting squeezed out by fly-by-night dot-commers paying ultra-high rents. His goal was to create a space where artists can be artists and build a sense of community, and he's done just that. Spanganga is an art gallery, theater, comedy club, venue for DJ parties and pretty much whatever else people want it to be. Check the website to see what it is today – and if it's even open.

ADDRESS 3376 19th street @ mission **TELEPHONE** 821-1102 **WEBSITE** www.spanganga.com **OPENING HOURS** check website **CREDIT CARDS** none **MUNI** 14, 33, 49

GALLERY SPANGANGA number 102 map G

notes

shopping   food & drink   nightlife   lodging   culture   various

SWINGING SAN FRANCISCO

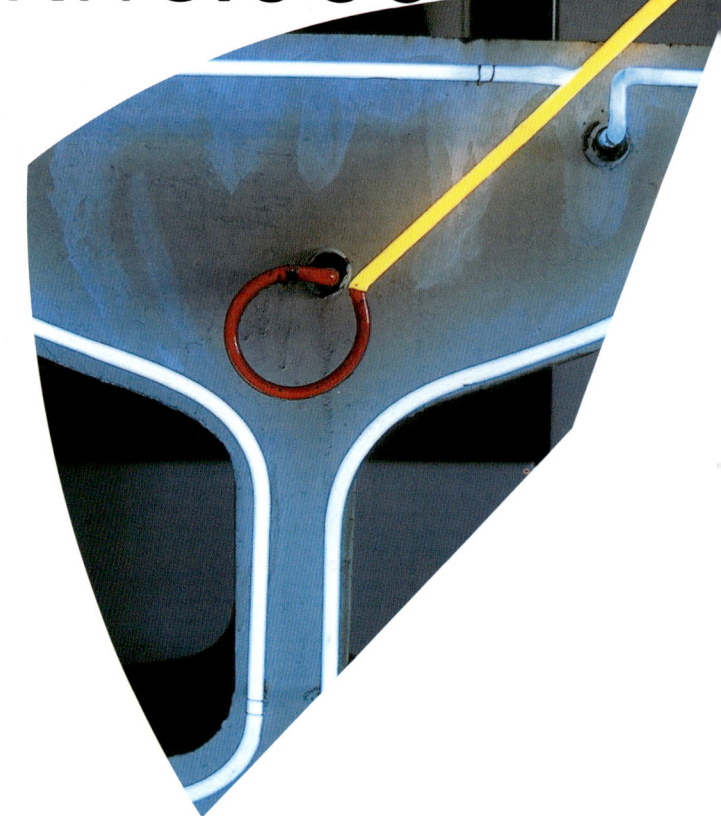

You know you live in a different world when, as you head home through the dawn-lit streets others are just getting their party night (or morning) started. Late-night/early-morning clubs in San Francisco are famous for their **Sunday morning dance parties**. And you thought Sunday morning was just for church.

Church is actually a good option on Sunday if you want to do a little dancing. Glide Memorial holds a **"Celebration"** every Sunday that will lift your spirits and get you shaking. These people can sing. If you meet up with someone on the street after a morning at Glide, chances are they'll be humming a tune and have a jitter in their feet.

A lot of the San Francisco music scene happens in **private**, behind **closed doors**. Local star Noe Venable says she often hears new bands in friends' living rooms. A fireplace, a guitar, a voice and an audience – what more could you need for an evening of music? Of course, you have to know the people who are hosting these concerts to know where to go, but if you stick around San Francisco long enough, you never know what you'll learn, who you'll meet or what you'll hear.

The music scene is more cooperative than competitive, say both Noe and local DJ celeb Sean Evans. Many bands record in their own studios or in studios owned by friends. There, they are not limited artistically and get valuable feedback from peers. If they do want to venture out into the world, there are so many **smaller venues** where live bands can play – not to mention open mic nights at some clubs – there's a good chance you'll hear them soon too.

If you haven't received the living room concert invitation just yet, head over to the Great **American Music Hall**. You'll be happy you did, no matter who's playing. Outside, the building doesn't look like much, but inside you'll do a double take. How could this crummy building be such a wonderland inside? This happens a lot in this city. Another world waits just through a set of doors. In San Francisco, you just need to open the right doors once in a while.

Local papers **SF Weekly** (www.sfweekly.com) and the **San Francisco Bay Guardian** (www.sfbg.com) are packed with information on the latest goings-on in music, theater, dance and anything else going on in the Bay Area. They're free – just look for them at

shopping   food & drink   nightlife   lodging   culture   various

newsstands. You'll also find out about seasonal festivals that might be going on. Keep an eye out for **Carnaval** in the Mission (May), the **Blues Festival** at Fort Mason (September) and the **Jazz Festival** (October).

There are also entire websites run by people who just try to keep up with what's going on in the music scene. DJ Sean Evans runs a site that will email you about the latest band, DJ, trend, or music-related news. The **information overload** can become overwhelming. So much good music and only two ears to hear it with... The question becomes not what to do, but when to find the time to do it all. It's time for **musical multi-tasking**.

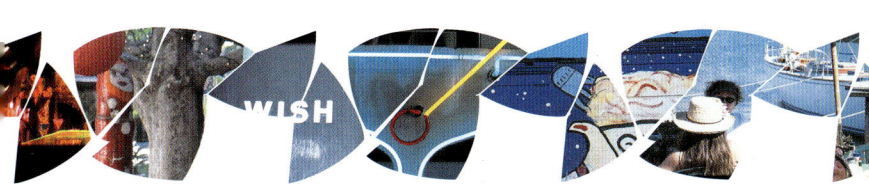

SWINGING SAN FRANCISCO

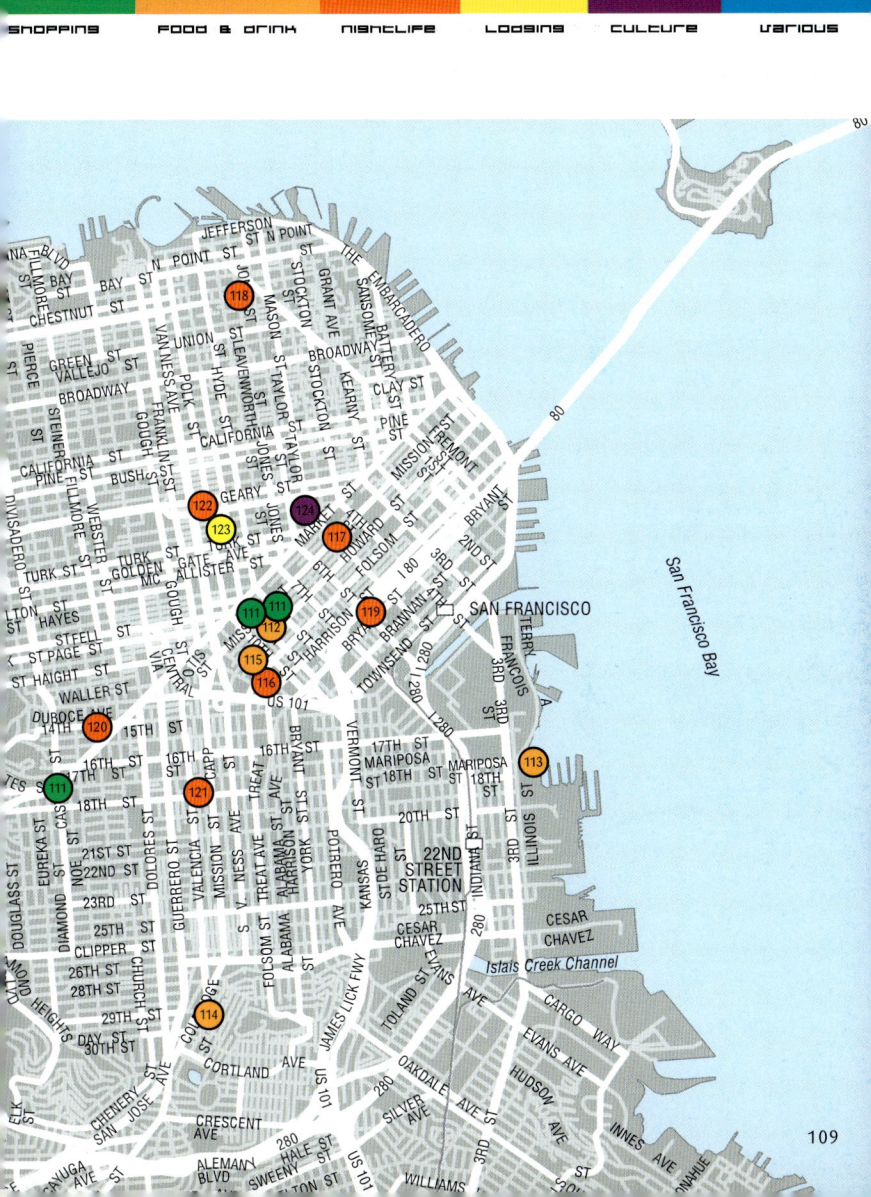

AMOEBA MUSIC number 110 map F

ADDRESS 1855 haight @ stanyan **TELEPHONE** 831-1200 **WEBSITE** www.amoebamusic.com **OPENING HOURS** daily 10am-10pm **CREDIT CARDS** visa, mastercard, amex **MUNI** 6, 7, 33, 43, n

Jazz, pop, lounge, indie, funk, rock and pretty much any other genre you've ever heard of is here and, if you're lucky, you'll even hear a live performance. You'll find new and used CDs alongside rare finds, vintage reissues, imports and even trade-ins – Amoeba buys old tunes for cash or store credit. It's a musical wonderland.

Can't keep up with the trends? Need to get out of those me-and-everyone-else khakis? Step into Rolo, where the staff knows how to make you hip. They'll dress you in Triple Five Soul, Fred Perry and G-Star or Stussy, D&G and Nike. The different locations have slightly different stock; for example, the 1301 Howard location is called the "Rolo Garage", where casual streetwear is king. At 1235 Howard you'll bag the higher-end threads. The Castro location even has markdown items. Shoes and skin care products for men are available too.

number 111 map G, H **ROLO**

ADDRESS locations (1) 1235 howard @ 9th street (2) 1301 howard @ 9th street (3) 2351 market @ castro
TELEPHONE (1) 355-1122 (2) 861-2097 (3) 431-4545 **WEBSITE** www.rolo.com **OPENING HOURS** (1+2) daily 11am-7pm (3) mon-sat 11am-8pm, sun 11pm-7pm **CREDIT CARDS** visa, mastercard, amex **MUNI** (1+2) 6, 7, 14, 19, 26, f, (3) 24, 35, 37, f, k, l, m

The top of the bar at this restaurant turns into a catwalk every night and your waiter/tress turns into a gender illusionist. As the lights get even dimmer, the music starts and the darling who just served you the ahi tuna burger gets up on stage to lip-synch like a madman (or woman). Try Trina's Pussycat or Karmina's Kiss if you get thirsty and be sure to order some dinner amidst the mayhem. The place gets even wilder downstairs at Club Boonda on Saturday nights.

ASIASF number 112 map H

ADDRESS 201 9th street @ howard **TELEPHONE** 255-2742 **WEBSITE** www.asiasf.com **OPENING HOURS** daily 10pm-2am **CREDIT CARDS** visa, mastercard, amex **PRICE** $12 **MUNI** 12, 14, 19, 26, f, j, k, l, m, n, bart: civic center

number 113 map H # THE RAMP

ADDRESS 855 china basin @ mariposa (3/4 mile south of pacbell park) **TELEPHONE** 621-2378 **OPENING HOURS** mon-fri 11:30am-3:30pm, sat-sun 8:30am-4pm **CREDIT CARDS** visa, mastercard **PRICE** $7 **MUNI** 15, 22

It's always a holiday at the Ramp, with its plastic chairs, picnic tables, little rippling waves, view of the bay and hearty diner food. The patio turns into a daytime dance party on weekend afternoons, to add to the festive ambiance. Come for the drinks, the view and the atmosphere.

You won't find spaghetti and seriously overgrown meatballs like this anywhere else. The aprons strung along a clothesline, dim lighting and 40-ounce beers make this place seem like a shack, but the spaghetti, extra-virgin olive oil and fresh mozzarella make it into a great restaurant. Add a DJ and you're good to go. Tip: The kitchen is open late and El Rio and other clubs are nearby.

EMMY'S
SPAGHETTI SHACK number 114 map G

ADDRESS 18 virginia @ mission **TELEPHONE** 206-2086 **OPENING HOURS** sun-thu 6pm-midnight, fri-sat 6pm-2am **CREDIT CARDS** none **PRICE** $9 **MUNI** 14, 24, 26, 67

SUSHI GROOVE SOUTH

number 115 map G

ADDRESS 1516 folsom @ 11th street **TELEPHONE** 503-1950 **OPENING HOURS** mon-wed 6pm-11:30pm, thu-sat 6pm-12:30pm **CREDIT CARDS** visa, mastercard, amex **PRICE** maki $6, entrée $9 **MUNI** 9, 12, 14, 19, 26

Grab an Asahi or a sake-tini in the front bar area and enjoy the vibe of the DJ before you get to the dining room. Once you're ready for some sushi, try the prosciutto-wrapped asparagus and ahi tartar on grilled toast or maybe the yellowtail "Jungle Roll" plump with papaya and tobiko. Before you leave, make sure to try the cold unfiltered sake. Also check out the sister location at 1916 Hyde @ Green in Russian Hill.

WISH number 116 map G

ADDRESS 1539 folsom @ 12th street **TELEPHONE** 278-9474 **WEBSITE** www.wishsf.com **OPENING HOURS** mon-sat 5pm-2am **CREDIT CARDS** visa, mastercard, amex **PRICE** no cover, cocktails $6 **MUNI** 9, 12

Maybe it's the warm crimson lighting that puts everyone in a cozy mood and makes everyone look beautiful or the long list of cocktails and the mix of post-work and pre-club folks living it up, but this is one happy place. At happy hour (from 5pm-8pm every night) things get even better. Make sure to try the house favorite, the Wish Twist ($6) with raspberry vodka and a sugar-rimmed glass. You'll hear house and European lounge grooves and a variety of DJs and never pay a cover charge.

Local nightlife veteran Audrey Joseph recently opened this art gallery/dance club and, as expected, it's a hit. On weeknights it's a gallery – with free shows on the first Tuesday and Wednesday of the month. The gallery transforms into a wild dance party on weekends. Hang out on the balcony for a view of the revelers below. If they seem to be staring at you, it's because to them you're a sexy silhouetted sweetie from above.

number 117 map C **MEZZANINE**

ADDRESS 444 jessie @ 5th street **TELEPHONE** 820-9669 **WEBSITE** www.mezzaninesf.com **OPENING HOURS** check website, sat 10pm-7am **CREDIT CARDS** none **PRICE** cover $7-15 **MUNI** 6, 7, 9, 14, 26, 66, 71

BIMBO'S 365 CLUB number 118 map C

ADDRESS 1025 columbus @ chestnut **TELEPHONE** 474-0365 **WEBSITE** www.bimbos365club.com **OPENING HOURS** check website for schedule **CREDIT CARDS** none **PRICE** check website **MUNI** 30, 39, powell/mason cable car

During the Great Depression, people needed a little pick-me-up and Bimbo was there to oblige. Agostino Giuntoli immigrated to San Francisco from Italy and worked as a janitor at the Palace Hotel before he and a pal started the 365 Club in 1931. Showgirls such as Rita Hayworth performed here while "The Girl in the Fishbowl" wowed patrons behind the bar (she's still there today). From concerts and private parties to swing and rock bands, if you can get tickets be sure to go.

You can come here on a Friday evening and not leave until Monday morning. Known for its early mornings as well as its late nights, The EndUp is still tops even after 30 years. Is it the music? The fireplace? The drinks? The pool table? The crowds? The heated patio? The waterfall? Yes.

number 119 map D **THE ENDUP**

ADDRESS 401 6th street @ harrison **TELEPHONE** 357-0827 **WEBSITE** www.theendup.com **OPENING HOURS** thu 10:30pm-4:30am, fri 10pm-6am, sat 6am-12pm & 10pm-4am, sun 6am-4am **CREDIT CARDS** none **PRICE** cover charge varies **MUNI** 9, 12, 27

Down a flight of stairs in a crimson underground world, Café du Nord offers a wide variety of live entertainment: jazz, rock, poetry readings, monologues, soul or cabaret. You never know what it might be, so check the schedule. Get there early, order a Blue Devil cocktail, find a cozy lounge chair and pretend you live around the corner.

CAFÉ DU NORD number 120 map G

ADDRESS 2170 market @ sanchez **TELEPHONE** 861-5016 **WEBSITE** www.cafedunord.com **OPENING HOURS** sun-tue 6pm-2am, wed-sat 4pm-2am **CREDIT CARDS** visa, mastercard **PRICE** cover $3-7 **MUNI** 8, 24, 37, f, k, l, m

number 121 map G # ELBO ROOM

ADDRESS 647 valencia @ 17th street **TELEPHONE** 552-7788 **WEBSITE** www.elbo.com **OPENING HOURS** daily 5pm-2am **CREDIT CARDS** none **PRICE** cover $3-7 **MUNI** 26, 33, 14, 49

Downstairs is a black and red bar, pool tables and a jukebox. Upstairs is a chaotic array of sweaty dancers in a confined space – but who's complaining? Experience great DJs or live music for a small cover charge, or take a break for a game of pool. On Sunday nights you get vintage dub sound, occasionally from old-school seven-inch singles. At happy hour, every day from 5pm-9pm, draft pints are $2 and cocktails are $1 off.

ADDRESS 859 o'farrell @ polk **TELEPHONE** 885-0750 **WEBSITE** www.gamh.com **OPENING HOURS** check schedule **CREDIT CARDS** visa, mastercard **PRICE** varies **MUNI** 19, 47, 49, 76

GREAT AMERICAN MUSIC HALL number 122 map C

With towering marble columns, elaborate balconies and 100 years of history, the Great American Music Hall is a peek into San Francisco's past. Today, the 5,000 square-foot hall fits 600 fans, who come to enjoy one of the best venues for live music and comedy. From Duke Ellington to Robin Williams, it's an honor to perform here and a pleasure to visit. Arrive when the doors open and have dinner – you'll get a seat, a view and a full belly.

Somehow, a motel that looks like it belongs on Route 66 ended up on the edge of the Tenderloin in downtown San Francisco. Step inside and all thoughts of dusty highways are gone. Hip new rock bands seem to like it here, perhaps because of the on-the-road motel feel. You can lounge around the pool for hours and listen to the hum of the crowd and the thump of the DJ inside the bar. Even if you don't sleep here, check out the ultra-trendy restaurant/club, Bambuddha Lounge, where you might have dinner next to a rock star (or at least a wannabe).

number 123 map C **PHOENIX HOTEL**

ADDRESS 601 eddy @ larkin **TELEPHONE** 776-1380 **WEBSITE** www.thephoenixhotel.com **CREDIT CARDS** visa, mastercard **PRICE** from $129 **MUNI** 19, 38, 47, 49

You don't need a reason to come to this church on Sunday morning – you need a reason not to. Glide is no ordinary church. People don't wait in line for half an hour to get into an ordinary church. You don't often hear, "you're a good dancer" whispered in the aisles of an ordinary church. The voices of the choir will lift your spirits so high that it will be a challenge to have a bad Sunday afternoon – or even a bad Monday. Get there by 10:15 for the 11am "Celebration."

GLIDE MEMORIAL CHURCH number 124 map D

ADDRESS 434 ellis @ taylor **TELEPHONE** 674-6000 **WEBSITE** www.glide.org
OPENING HOURS sun 9am & 11am **MUNI** 2, 3, 4, 27, 38

shopping   food & drink   nightlife   lodging   culture   various

number 125 map E LINDY IN THE PARK

ADDRESS golden gate park, music concourse, near fulton @ 8th avenue **WEBSITE** www.lindyinthepark.com
OPENING HOURS sun 10am-12:30pm **MUNI** 21, 44, n

Every Sunday in Golden Gate Park, dozens of people get together to dance the "Lindy Hop." A dance from the 1920s, the Lindy is swing dancing at its finest. What started in 1996 with just a boom box and a few swing dancers has evolved into a weekly event complete with DJs and a sound system. People of all ages come out to swing on nice days and everyone is welcome to dance or just sit and watch.

THE VALENCIA CORRIDOR

Many neighborhoods outside downtown change often. People move in and out, things get better or worse (depending on your perspective) and "new" neighborhoods are formed. Hayes Valley took an earthquake to get it going and for the **Valencia Corridor** it took the dot-com boom.

With **rents skyrocketing** in most of the city in the 1990s, people who were determined to live in the city of San Francisco were naturally guided to where the prices – and the hills – were a little less steep. The west edge of the Mission bordering Noe Valley started sprouting trendy restaurants, odd-but-somehow-useful shops, and bars and clubs for those hip young folks moving in. Second-hand but cool furniture shops sprang up. Bakeries with designer chefs, bistros with valet parking and clubs with fancy and pricey cocktails moved in. Latino shops, artists' studios and some of the local color and vibrancy was pushed out, but in came a new vibrancy of a different flavor.

Many of the dot-com businesses have now gone broke, but those former dot-commers still try to blend in: they ride bikes to work now, their fortunes fitting into piggy banks, and keep hoping that rents will come down. Journalist David Brooks calls these middle-of-two-worlds folks "Bobos" or the **bohemian bourgeoisie**. Caught between enjoying life with the best of them and occasionally earning a wad of cash, they live on the edge.

Mission Street still holds as much flavor as a **savory fish taco**, and with the **colorful murals** on many of its walls and **tasty taquerias** on the corners, there's no doubt that the Latino flavor of the Mission will remain. So will the new Valencia Street and the older Mission Street be able to coexist? Only time will tell.

The two areas do seem to run on different schedules. Things didn't slowly make their way to **Valencia** – they shot up overnight. There are now so many **restaurants, bookstores, cafés, antique stores, furniture shops, bars, clubs** and hangouts that you wonder how they all survive. (The answer is, they don't.) With such good food on the next block, each restaurant has to come up with the freshest ideas; each club has to spin the hottest music; each store has to stock the newest products. As a result, you – the consumer-eater-shopper-clubgoer – get the best of the best.

Thanks in part to the lower rents, shop and restaurant owners can be more creative and take more risks. There are shops along the street that you may not understand. Have a look inside and decide for yourself whether it's an **art gallery** or a garage, a bookstore or a **pirate's eye-patch** shop, a gardening store or a **voodoo magic palace**.

Have a walk along the whole street, all the way from Market Street to around 26th Street and see what you find. New shops, galleries, restaurants and bars sprout up all the time, so keep an eye open for the latest hotspot. The buildings along the way aren't exactly featured in "Architectural Digest," but it's what's inside that counts, right?

When you've had your fill of thrift stores and great food, nearby **Dolores Park** (dolores @ 18th Street) is a favorite sunny-day hangout. The "microclimate" here often has warmer temperatures than other parts of town (San Francisco has many neighborhoods, and the hills often make their weather slightly different, even just a few blocks away). Frisbee, dogs, kids, BBQs, moms, tennis courts and grass everywhere make this a local picnic favorite. Pick up some snacks at Bi-Rite and spend some time **sitting doing nothing**.

THE VALENCIA CORRIDOR

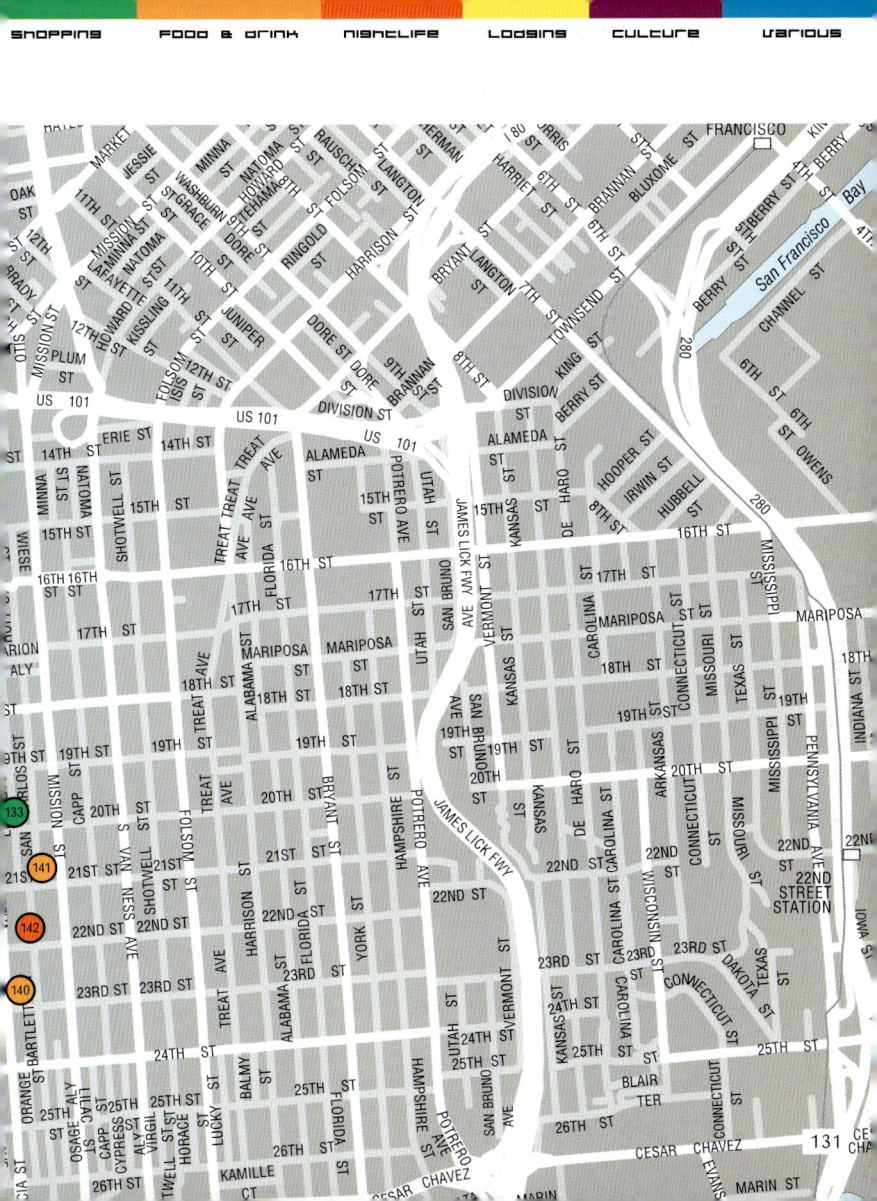

X21 number 132 map G

ADDRESS 890 valencia @ 20th street **TELEPHONE** 647-4211 **WEBSITE** www.x21modern.com **OPENING HOURS** mon-thu 12pm-6pm, fri, sun 12pm-7pm, sat 12pm-8pm **CREDIT CARDS** visa, mastercard **MUNI** 14, 26, 49, j

Vintage office furniture, steel lamps, industrial design, glass, ceramics ... you'll find pretty much anything here. None of it is new, but all of it is ultra-cool in a retro way. The store specializes in reconditioning steel or metal, polishing it up to look as good as new, or in this case, as good as old. The stuff is so authentic that they also run a prop business for movie and TV production companies. Don't miss the basement, which is even bigger and full of bargains.

Subterranean has everything you need to be who you want to be: Lo-rise and hi-rise boots by Sendra and sandals by Fornarina, 80s retro Adidas and the latest by Fly London. Are you a Frye Daisy Duke or more of a Fornarina Snob? Maybe you're a straightforward Vans Jane Doe or a wild Sendra girl. Be whoever you want to be and put your best foot forward.

SUBTERRANEAN SHOE ROOM

number 133 map G

ADDRESS 877 valencia @ 20th street **TELEPHONE** 401-9504 **WEBSITE** www.subshoeroom.com **OPENING HOURS** daily 12pm-7pm **CREDIT CARDS** visa, mastercard, amex **MUNI** 14, 26, 49, j

You can still get an iron-on T-shirt at Retro Fit. They have over 150 transfers to choose from – from the forever-hip Atari logo to rocking 80s Van Halen shirts and ever-cool "Love Boat"-designs. There are plenty of shirt styles too: baseball jerseys, camisoles, customary Beefy-Ts, or you can bring your own. The store also carries a variety of other hats and shirts, but it'll be hard to take your eyes off that star-studded wall of history. One of the most popular is child-star and former candidate for California governor, Gary Coleman, saying "Whatchoo talkin'bout?"

RETRO FIT VINTAGE number 134 map G

ADDRESS 910 valencia @ 20th street **TELEPHONE** 550-1530 **OPENING HOURS** sun, mon, wed 12pm-6pm, thu 1:30pm-7pm, fri 12pm-7pm, sat 12pm-8pm **CREDIT CARDS** visa, mastercard, amex **MUNI** 14, 26, 49, j

number 135 map G # ZEITGEIST

ADDRESS 199 valencia @ duboce **TELEPHONE** 255-7505 **OPENING HOURS** daily 9am-2am, happy hour 9am-8pm **CREDIT CARDS** none **PRICE** $5 **MUNI** 26, 49, f

There are so many pitchers of beer out on the picnic tables on a sunny day that you might think they're mandatory. Bicycles and motorcycles rule this place on the weekends, but anyone who's interested in a casual, backyard atmosphere with BBQed burgers and sausages, 30 beers on tap, 30 more in bottles and enough pitchers for everyone, is welcome. Try the BBQ ribs.

Founders Elisabeth Prueitt and Chad Robertson bake all day, so the Niman Ranch smoked ham "croque monsieur" was made minutes ago, not hours ago. The couple started this bakery in pleasant Point Reyes, an hour's drive from the city, and only recently opened this urban outpost. Aside from the lick-your-lips-luscious pastries, they also have hot pressed sandwiches like the Redwood Hill Goat, with soft local goat cheese.

TARTINE BAKERY number 136 map G

ADDRESS 600 guerrero @ 18th street **TELEPHONE** 487-2600 **OPENING HOURS** mon 8am-2pm, tue-fri 7:30am-7pm, sat 8am-7pm, sun 10am-6pm **CREDIT CARDS** visa, mastercard, amex **PRICE** $6 **MUNI** 14, 26, 33, 49, j

number 137 map G # DELFINA

ADDRESS 3621 18th @ dolores **TELEPHONE** 552-4055 **OPENING HOURS** fri-sat 5:30pm-11pm, sun-thu 5:30pm-10pm **CREDIT CARDS** visa, mastercard **PRICE** $15 **MUNI** 14, 26, 33, 49, j

Delfina is food pure and simple, serving savory dishes made with care. The atmosphere is trendy but not snobby, the tables are snug but not cramped and the noise level is loud but not thunderous. Try the grilled calamari over tiny white beans or a flatiron steak with fries. Save room for some Scharffen Berger chocolate cake with "crème anglaise".

You don't need to dress up in your Sunday best to enjoy tea and scones at this Mission District eatery – in fact you don't even need to come on Sunday. Famous cucumber and cream cheese tea sandwiches, lemon curd, crumpets, and salads are on the menu alongside shepherd's pie and sausage rolls, for those who like their afternoon snacks a little heartier. The teacups don't match, and neither do the chairs, but it all boils down to tasty tea for two.

LOVEJOY'S TEA ROOM number 138 map G

ADDRESS 1351 church @ clipper **TELEPHONE** 648-5895 **OPENING HOURS** wed-sun 11am-6pm **CREDIT CARDS** visa, mastercard **PRICE** high tea $15 **MUNI** 26, j

number 139 map G # LUNA PARK

ADDRESS 694 valencia @ 18th street **TELEPHONE** 553-8584 **WEBSITE** www.lunaparksf.com **OPENING HOURS** daily 11am-2:30pm & 5:30pm-10:30pm **CREDIT CARDS** visa, mastercard, amex **PRICE** $13 **MUNI** 14, 26, 33, 49, j

Hide away in a cozy booth – even cozier in the back with private curtains and a dimmer switch – or sit at the bar with candles and cocktails. The high walls are slathered in a deep red paint that creates a mood of hip tranquility. The Italian-esque food is fresh, cooked just right and plentiful. Start off with a volcano fondue of goat cheese, garlic bread and sliced apples. The broccoli rabe is also delish.

LAST SUPPER CLUB number 140 map G

ADDRESS 1199 valencia @ 23rd street **TELEPHONE** 695-1199 **WEBSITE** www.lastsupperclubsf.com **OPENING HOURS** daily 11am-3pm & 5:30pm-10:30pm **CREDIT CARDS** visa, mastercard, amex **PRICE** $14 **MUNI** 14, 26, 49, j, bart: 24th & mission

Step off busy Valencia Street and into an Italian restaurant like nothing in North Beach. No street salesmen trying to get you inside, no cheesy bottles of Chianti strapped to plastic grapes. This is the Italy you hoped for. People don't just eat here, they seem to live here… they blend into the scenery and read a newspaper at the bar or savor a glass of wine by the window. Huge steel pots hang above the half-open kitchen, where the chef strikes an even balance between organic produce and real butter. This is the home you wished you lived in.

Lounge on the outdoor patio on a warm summer evening and watch a classic such as Fellini's La Dolce Vita projected on the patio wall. Sip wine, talk about vineyards and literature, snack on bistro food and try to imagine when life was better than this. You'll be hard-pressed to think of a time…

number 141 map G **FOREIGN CINEMA**

ADDRESS 2534 mission @ 21st street **TELEPHONE** 648-7600 **WEBSITE** www.foreigncinema.com **OPENING HOURS** tue-sat 6pm-2am, sun 11am-2am **CREDIT CARDS** visa, mastercard, amex **PRICE** $18 **MUNI** 14, 49

The oil paintings, the red velvet curtains, the stuffed deer head and the $1 bottles of Pabst Blue Ribbon during happy hour (mon-thu 6pm-8pm) all make you feel like you're at a 1970s costume party. But this is the Make-Out Room, where kitsch is still king. If the disco ball gets to be too much, get cozy in one of the red booths and make the place live up to its name. If you're feelin less amorous, you can still enjoy the hip DJs and live bands.

MAKE-OUT ROOM number 142 map G

ADDRESS 3225 22nd street @ bartlett **TELEPHONE** 647-2888 **WEBSITE** www.makeoutroom.com **OPENING HOURS** daily 6pm-2am **CREDIT CARDS** none **PRICE** $6 **MUNI** 14, 26, 48, 49, j, bart: 24th & mission

number 143 map G # HOTEL TROPICANA

ADDRESS 663 valencia @ 18th street **TELEPHONE** 701-7666 **WEBSITE** www.thehoteltropicana.com **CREDIT CARDS** visa, mastercard **PRICE** from $79 **MUNI** 14, 26, 33, 49, j

If you feel at home in the Valencia scene, you might want to sleep close by. Bright and cheery, young and alive, the Tropicana is not exactly the Ritz Carlton, but you can have dinner at Delfina, drinks at the Elbo Room and wake up within walking distance of Tartine Bakery. More of a hostel than a hotel, you're bound to meet up with interesting travelers from around the world.

HAYES VALLEY

shopping • food & drink • nightlife • lodging • culture • various

If you know where to look, you'll find signs of an old freeway that used to pass almost directly over this part of town. The freeway had the personality of most downtown mega-structures: **massive concrete pillars, traffic congestion** and noise and **areas where the sun never shone**. When the 1989 earthquake hit, the freeway was so badly damaged that it was torn down.

With the cement and tarmac gone, new shops and restaurants began to pop up along Hayes Street. People started to move into a now-quiet neighborhood where thousands of cars had once passed every day. What used to be just a commuter part of town suddenly became a **destination**.

Between 1993 and 1998, at least 23 businesses opened up along two blocks of Hayes Street. There are now so many **boutiques** that you might forget which one you're in. You'll discover **funky jewelry shops**, new and used clothing stores, **design studios** where you can actually afford to buy the art and cafés cozy enough to spend all day in. Get a haircut, try on a pair of shoes, sip cappuccino or just stroll around under the lush trees and make yourself at home.

Many people have already made **Hayes Valley** home, and there have been a lot of changes. One local resident said there used to be a bar on Hayes Street where, when a cop walked in, you could hear the guns drop on to the wooden benches. Now the only thing that drops to the floor is a cell phone. Community events such as evening block parties seem a sign that the neighborhood is working together to make the place safe and fun for everyone.

Well, not exactly everyone. In 2003, the neighbors voted to keep Starbucks from moving in. Petitions, posters in shop windows and a grass-roots campaign held the chain at bay and now you **won't find any sign of a Starbucks** on Hayes Street. In fact, you won't find signs of many chain stores on Hayes, as they're just not welcome. Hayes Valley started as a community effort and residents want to keep it that way; it seems to be working, too.

On a map of San Francisco, the neighborhood makes sense. It's close enough to downtown to walk, yet near many public transportation lines. The **opera** is nearby, the **Herbst Theatre** is just down the street and SoMa is just a zig-zag away. Hayes Valley even has one of those famous "microclimates" where the sun shines more than elsewhere (which is

why it's always a good idea, ANY time of year, to carry a light jacket or sweater in San Francisco). It took planning, hard work and an earthquake to make this neighborhood what it is today.

In 2003, the rest of the freeway that went along nearby Octavia Street was demolished. There are now plans in the works for a whole new neighborhood project called **"Octavia Boulevard."** Keep your eyes open for falling cement structures and sprouting new neighborhoods.

Hayes Valley is along Hayes Street between Franklin and Laguna Streets.

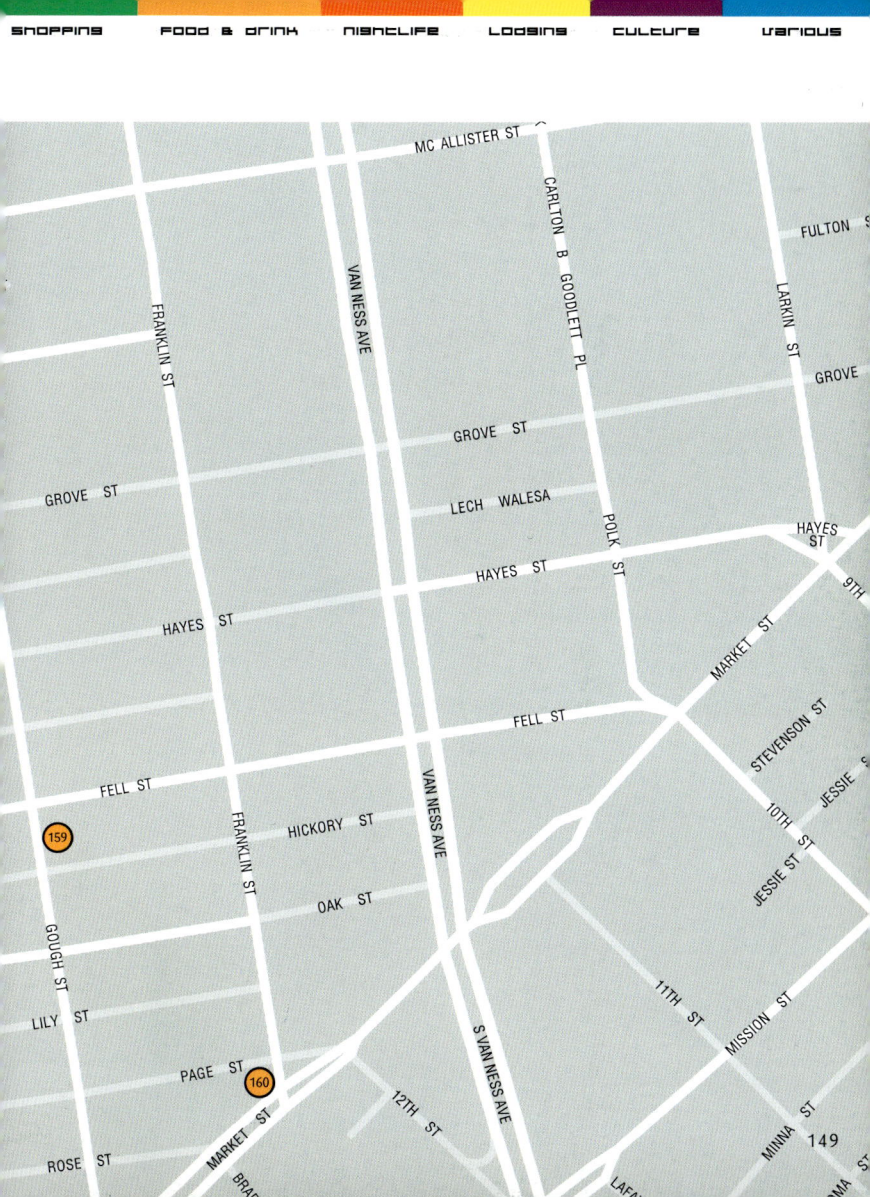

ALABASTER number 150 map C

ADDRESS 597 hayes @ laguna **TELEPHONE** 558-0587 **WEBSITE** www.alabastersf.com **OPENING HOURS** tue-sat 11am-6pm, sun 12pm-5pm **CREDIT CARDS** visa, amex, mastercard **MUNI** 5, 6, 7, 21, 47, 49, 71

There's something pure and soothing about this shop. You can look around at the work from small designers in Italy, France and Spain, but it's only when you look up into the white silk lanterns that you learn where the pearly, silvery, warm light comes from. A small selection of books and music snuggles next to Murano glass and Fortuny purses just the way it would in someone's home. Because there are only a few books and CDs, they'll catch your eye, as you can tell they've been chosen with as much care and consideration as everything else here.

shopping   food & drink   nightlife   lodging   culture   various

Metal and glass spice racks that look like little washing machines at a laundromat are a good example of the kinds of designs born in this store. You might find something like this at Crate & Barrel, but not for another five years. This store is cutting edge, but in an affordable price range.

ADDRESS 555 hayes @ laguna **TELEPHONE** 701-7767 **WEBSITE** www.propeller-sf.com **OPENING HOURS** tue-sat 11am-7pm, sun 12pm-5pm **CREDIT CARDS** visa, mastercard, amex **MUNI** 5, 6, 7, 21, 47, 49, 71

number 151 map C   # PROPELLER

The staff at Alla Prima knows lingerie. The focus is on fit and form and the staff members will personally assist you in finding what works best for your individual shape. European lingerie lines like Eres and La Perla are available in abundance, but there are also a few American designers as well. There's also a selection of European swimwear, loungewear, cover-ups and camisoles. The hardwood floors and soft colors make this a cozy, intimate boutique.

ALLA PRIMA number 152 map D

ADDRESS two locations (1) 539 hayes @ octavia (2) 1420 grant @ green **TELEPHONE** 397-4077 **WEBSITE** www.allaprima.net **OPENING HOURS** mon-sat 11am-7pm, sun 12pm-5pm **CREDIT CARDS** visa, mastercard, amex **MUNI** (1) 5, 6, 7, 21, 47, 49, 71 (2) 15, 30, 41

BULO

number 153 map C

ADDRESS three locations (1) women 418 hayes @ gough (2) men 437-a hayes @ octavia (3) 3044 fillmore @ union **TELEPHONE** 864-3244 **WEBSITE** www.buloshoes.com **OPENING HOURS** mon-sat 11am-6:30pm, sun 12-6pm **CREDIT CARDS** visa, mastercard, amex **MUNI** (1&2) 5, 6, 7, 21, 47, 49, 71 (3) 22, 41, 45

Italian shoe designers such as Roberto del Carlo, Aeffe and J. Hen always stay one step ahead of American style. If you like to be ahead of the trends as well, check in with one of Bulo's stores. The shoes are stylish, imported and undoubtedly Italian.

FLIGHT 001 number 154 map C

ADDRESS 525 hayes @ octavia **TELEPHONE** 487-1001 **WEBSITE** www.flight001.com **OPENING HOURS** mon-sat 11am-7pm, sun 11am-6pm **CREDIT CARDS** visa, mastercard, amex **MUNI** 5, 6, 7, 21, 47, 49, 71

Named after PanAm's first commercial flight around the world in 1942, this shop spans the generations. Leaf through books to see what air hostesses have worn through the years or try to decide which neon-colored luggage tag you should get so you can see your bags from three claim areas away. There are tons of useful items here you may wish you packed, done with so much style that you will feel the need to replace the items you did pack.

Head to the back of this shop to see local artist Andrea Süss create her handmade jewelry, or just browse the skirts, handbags, trousers and belts that seem to be overflowing from the shelves around the store. Owner and leather designer Heidi Weiner is one of only a handful of on-site leather designers in the city. She has her own line of leather products and can also restore your well-aged jackets to their sprightly young selves again.

ADDRESS 542 hayes @ octavia **TELEPHONE** 552-6468 **WEBSITE** www.lava9.com **OPENING HOURS** mon-sat 12pm-7pm, sun 12pm-5pm **CREDIT CARDS** visa, mastercard, amex **MUNI** 5, 6, 7, 21, 47, 49, 71

number 155 map C **LAVA 9**

This store is filled with jewelry, handbags, watches, scented candles, bath products, small pieces of furniture and an international collection of housewares. Aromatherapy designers with names like "Bazaar des Senteurs" and "We Live Like This" showcase their extraordinary products here. Apparel designers such as Lemon Twist, Barbara Bui, Daryl K, and jil stuart also show off their well-cut, body-smart clothing. Everything here works well and looks good.

BUU number 156 map C

ADDRESS 506 hayes @ octavia **TELEPHONE** 626-1503 **OPENING HOURS** mon-wed 12pm-7pm, thu-sat 11am-7pm, sun 12pm-6pm **CREDIT CARDS** visa, mastercard, amex **MUNI** 5, 6, 7, 21, 47, 49, 71

number 157 map C **VELVET DA VINCI**

ADDRESS 508 hayes @ octavia **TELEPHONE** 626-7478 **WEBSITE** www.velvetdavinci.com **OPENING HOURS** tue-sat 12pm-6pm, sun 12pm-4pm **CREDIT CARDS** visa, mastercard, amex **MUNI** 5, 6, 7, 21, 47, 49, 71

Pioneers Mike Holmes and Elizabeth Shypertt opened their contemporary art, jewelry and metal works shop in 1991 when Hayes Street was just a string of empty storefronts in the shadow of the freeway. Now Holmes and Shypertt represent over 50 artists from around the world. You won't find these pieces anywhere else and you'll love the rings, brooches, necklaces, tiaras, kinetic sculpture and life-size wire people you'll find at Velvet da Vinci.

ADDRESS 525 laguna @ hayes **TELEPHONE** 252-9289 **WEBSITE** www.suppenkuche.com **OPENING HOURS** mon-sat 5pm-10pm, sun 10am-2:30pm **CREDIT CARDS** visa, mastercard, amex **PRICE** $13 **MUNI** 5, 6, 7, 21, 47, 49, 71

SUPPENKÜCHE number 158 map C

Although the bench-style seating at Suppenküche ("soup kitchen" in German) won't guarantee you'll get to know your neighbors, it will guarantee you'll hear them. The California influence on the German fare ensures that the kitchen goes easy on creams, butters and fats, but not on taste. Sit under a vaulted ceiling and make your way through German rye, fresh pea soup, spaetzle (noodle dumplings) and veal meatballs. Your only challenge will be which of the 18 German beers to pick. Try a few of these hearty German brews and your neighbors might just get to know you.

shopping   food & drink   nightlife   lodging   culture   various

You don't have to speak French to savor the fresh baguettes, croissants, salads and soups here but it doesn't hurt, since you'll hear a lot of it. The French-American School is right next door, and at lunch many French and French-Canadian residents swoop in to chat, reminisce and savor the flavor of back home.

number 159 map G **CAFÉ TARTINE**

ADDRESS 244 gough @ fell **TELEPHONE** 553-4595 **OPENING HOURS** mon-fri 7am-5pm, sat 8am-5pm
CREDIT CARDS visa, mastercard, amex **PRICE** $6 **MUNI** 6, 7, 21, 47, 49, 71

Not many places can boast the sheer square footage of windows that this corner location can. Make sure you're not on the outside of all that glass. Zuni is one of those places where you walk by and wish you were already inside sipping wine, eating fresh oysters, munching on crunchy shoestring fries and imagining yourself as the star of a television ad where everyone is happy and beautiful all the time.

ADDRESS 1658 market @ franklin **TELEPHONE** 552-2522 **OPENING HOURS** tue-sat 11:30am-midnight, sun 11am-11pm **CREDIT CARDS** visa, mastercard, amex **PRICE** $20 **MUNI** 6, 7, 26, 47, 49, 71, f, bart: civic center

ZUNI CAFÉ number 160 map G

number 161 map C **PLACE PIGALLE**

ADDRESS 520 hayes @ octavia **TELEPHONE** 552-2671 **WEBSITE** www.place-pigalle.com **OPENING HOURS** thu-sat 4pm-2am, sun-wed 4pm-midnight **CREDIT CARDS** visa, mastercard **PRICE** $3 **MUNI** 21, 47, 49

You might not expect a place like this to have wine, but it does. It also has live jazz, literary and performance art events as well as pool tables, tap beer and a happy hour that should keep you going strong. The pool table in the back has posted warnings about "local pool sharks," so beware.

FRJTZ number 162 map C

ADDRESS 579 hayes @ laguna **TELEPHONE** 864-7654 **WEBSITE** www.frjtzfries.com **OPENING HOURS** mon-thu 9am-10pm, fri-sat 10am-midnight, sun 10am-9pm **CREDIT CARDS** visa, mastercard, amex **PRICE** $5 **MUNI** 5, 6, 7, 21, 47, 49, 71

When you taste the thick frites with the skin still on them served in a paper cone, you might think you're in Belgium. But with a selection of sauces including pesto mayo, Vietnamese chili ketchup and spicy peanut yogurt, you'll know you're in California. The restaurant also serves crepes, sandwiches and salads and has somehow even managed to squeeze a DJ spinning table into this narrow corridor of space. Every Friday night, DJ Frjtz spins his eclectic music. Head back to the relaxed garden patio and order yourself a Chimay, Hoegaarden or Duvel just to keep with the spirit of things.

shopping   food & drink   nightlife   Lodging   culture   various

Stay in this Victorian bed and breakfast if you'd rather live like a local than a tourist. There's a nice common kitchen area and a cozy parlor with a corner view of Hayes Street, and all this is within walking distance of the Opera House, Symphony Hall, Civic Center, zillions of restaurants and everything Hayes Valley has to offer. After a tough day walking through galleries and eating fine food, return to the inn for a massage and body treatment, offered on the premises.

number 163 map C **HAYES VALLEY INN**

ADDRESS 417 gough @ hayes **TELEPHONE** 431-9131, 800-930-7999 **WEBSITE** www.hayesvalleyinn.com
CREDIT CARDS visa, mastercard, amex **PRICE** from $66 **MUNI** 5, 6, 7, 21, 47, 49, 71

This place is many things in one. It's a salon, massage parlor and occasional party spot with mirrors shaped like rocket ships, grooving music and a head massage with every shampoo. The atmosphere is hip but relaxed, professional but friendly. Have a cup of coffee, chat a while and watch your hair being transformed in front of your eyes.

OXENROSE number 164 map C

ADDRESS 500 hayes @ octavia **TELEPHONE** 252-9723 **OPENING HOURS** mon-fri 11am-8pm, sat 10am-7pm, sun 12pm-7pm **CREDIT CARDS** visa, mastercard **PRICE** from $40, depending on stylist **MUNI** 21, 47, 49

notes

BOHEMIA, CALIFORNIA

Haight Ashbury - or the Haight - and **North Beach** are two centers of bohemian life in San Francisco, both past and present. The Haight had its hippie heyday in the 60s while North Beach hosted the Beatnik generation in the 50s. Some people might say that most of San Francisco has a bohemian vibe, and that it's not confined to certain neighborhoods. There is a certain reputation here for enjoying life that San Franciscans must keep up, after all.

While the world was going nuts with e-everything and i-anything, the **dot-com explosion** had different effects on different people in and around San Francisco. Rents increased and the bohemian crowd was often squeezed out – as far out as Oregon. For a few years there, if you weren't making **millions of dollars** with your IPO, you really didn't exist. You were nobody and you also had more trouble paying the rent. Things have started to get back to normal, except that rents haven't come down much and the cost of purchasing a place in San Francisco still only goes in an upward direction.

Bohemians **rich and poor** love San Francisco anyway, and always find their way back to the city or as close as they can get to it. In the Haight, North Beach and the Mission, artists are coming back as landlords realize that lower rent is better than no rent. Artist studios are opening up again, smaller theaters are returning and there is new hope for bohemia.

While the Haight used to be a true hippie haven, it's now just somewhat of a hippie haven with shopping. **Upper Haight** (Haight Street from Stanyan to Masonic) is loaded with shops, restaurants, bookstores, pizza joints, music shops and used-clothing stores. Grunge still classifies as high fashion here and young people usually outnumber old. The streets are bustling with all sorts of folks, especially on weekend afternoons. Still, things have changed quite a bit since names like "Rainbow" were tops in baby-naming books. Although there are still **head shops** and **record stores** where you can find vinyl, the famed corner of Haight and Ashbury now has a GAP and a Ben and Jerry's.

Have a walk around upper Haight and get lost in the shops, stop for a bite to eat at one of numerous cafés and do some people-watching. Upper Haight is also the gateway to the **Golden Gate Park**, where you can rent bikes and rollerblades and cruise the greenery. This area used to be "out in the country" for San Franciscans of yesteryear, but now you don't have to worry about getting back to the "city."

Lower Haight (Haight Street from Divisadero to Webster) is more local, less touristy and known to have some of the best eateries in the city (Indian Oven and Thep Phanom). Rosamunde **Sausage Grill** & Toronado Pub is a local hangout and a good spot to chill out with a sausage and watch a sports event on TV. Head across the street to **The Mad Dog in the Fog**, where you can often find European footballers watching late-night

soccer matches. This is a great place to live, not too far from the center of the city but not so close to be too busy and crowded with tourists.

North Beach has a more suave, refined, Italian style than the Haight, but the artistic and literary interests are still there, squeezed in between the tourists. North Beach has a longer history than the Haight and has managed to stay popular with a wide variety of people: old-timer locals, young ones living the lively life, and, of course, Italians. In the late 1800s, Italians poured into the area and this became the Latin Quarter of town. Joe DiMaggio grew up here and is a long-time local hero. Then **Jack Kerouac** and **Allen Ginsberg** came into town in the 50s and North Beach became Beatnik Central. They brought not only their literature, but their lifestyle ... oh-so San Francisco.

Both neighborhoods are full of surprises and just walking around them is interesting. Stray from the main drags (Haight Street and Columbus Avenue) to get a more local perspective. You'll discover focaccia shops that only sell focaccia or, near the Haight, old Victorian homes resting behind the shade of trees at Golden Gate Park.

BOHEMIA, CALIFORNIA

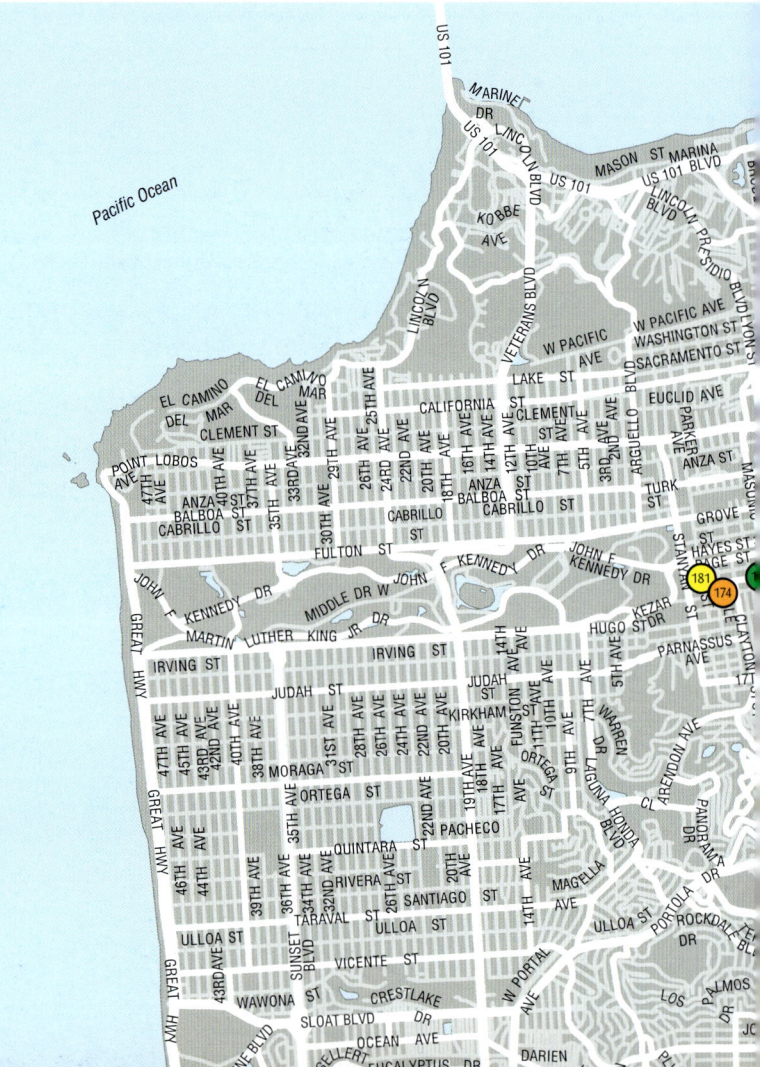

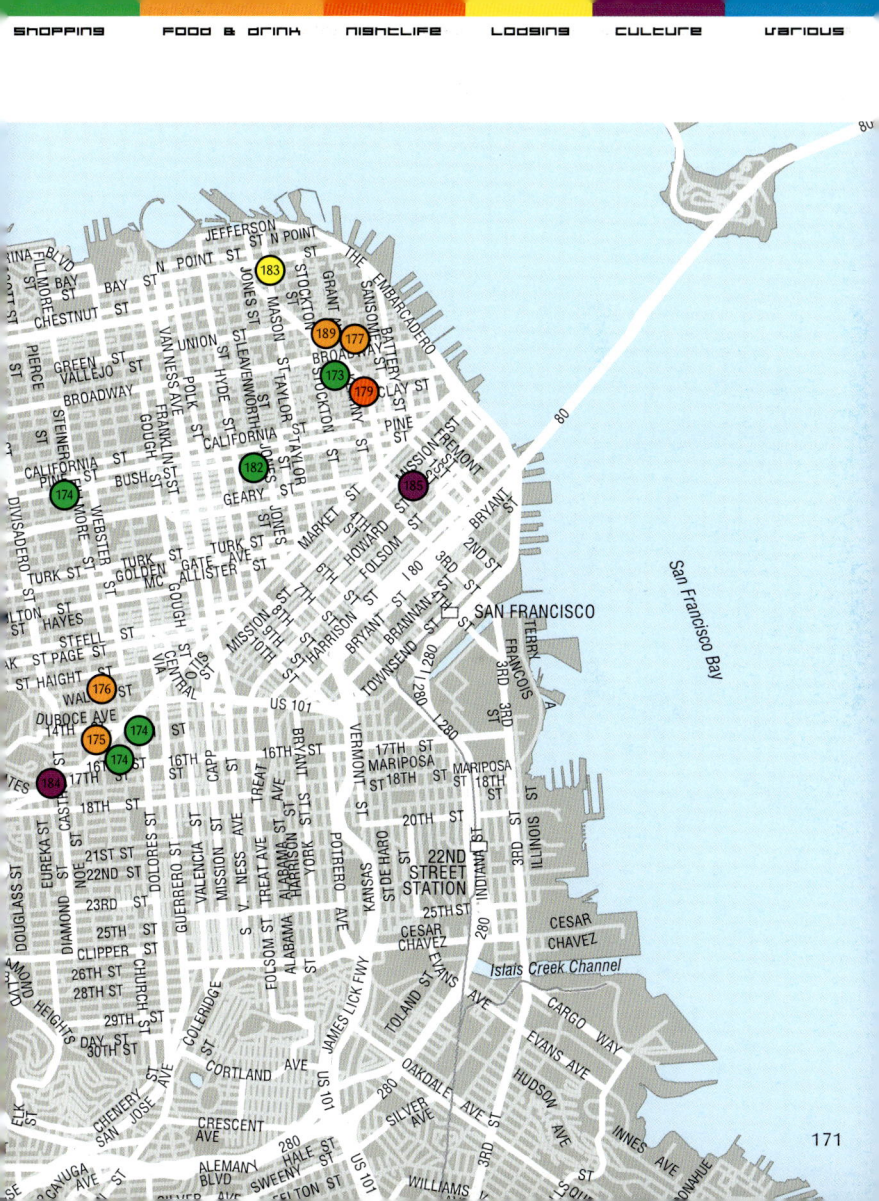

When you see the sign that says, "No pictures or video! We WILL take your camera!" you know you need to go in. Whether you're throwing a party, going to a party or just want to be a one-person party, this is the place to explore. Almost all of the clothing is hand-made by the staff and if they don't have it, you can bet your feather boa they'll custom make it for you. From lacy lingerie to wild wigs, Hawaiian men's club shirts to hip-hugging rhinestone spandex shorts, there's a unique fashion here for every occasion you can imagine – and some you can't!

PIEDMONT BOUTIQUE number 172 map F

ADDRESS 1452 haight @ masonic **TELEPHONE** 864-8075 **WEBSITE** www.piedmontsf.com **OPENING HOURS** daily 11am-7pm **CREDIT CARDS** visa, mastercard, amex **MUNI** 6, 7, 33, 43, 66, 71

number 173 map D # CITY LIGHTS BOOKSTORE

ADDRESS 261 columbus @ broadway **TELEPHONE** 362-8193 **WEBSITE** www.citylights.com **OPENING HOURS** daily 10am-midnight **CREDIT CARDS** visa, mastercard, amex **MUNI** 15, 30, 45

Not too many bookstores in the world have sections called "Muckraking," "Stolen Continents" or "Situationism." But not many bookstores have had the history that City Lights has had. Founded by poet Lawrence Ferlinghetti in 1953 to provide cheap paperbacks to returning WWII soldiers, this has been an influential independent bookseller ever since. Two visiting Italian students were so impressed that when they returned to Florence they opened up a sister City Lights. Make sure you find the section called "Evidence."

"No, no, definitely no, yes, no, whoa, yes. Thanks," the salesgirl says to a walk-in seller. Crossroads is picky when it comes to buying clothes from the public. That selective standard means the fashions it carries aren't the same as most left-in-the-alley thrift stores. The stores also buys from wholesalers, so there's a chance they'll have multiple sizes of a piece. Each of its San Francisco addresses caters to its own neighborhood.

CROSSROADS
TRADING COMPANY number 174 map B, C, E, F, G

ADDRESS four locations (1) 1519 haight @ ashbury (2) 555 irving @ 7th street (3) 2123 market @ church (4) 1901 fillmore @ bush **TELEPHONE** (1) 355-0555 (2) 681-0100 (3) 552-8740 (4) 775-8885 **WEBSITE** www.crossroadstrading.com **OPENING HOURS** mon-thu 11am-7pm, fri-sat 11am-8pm, sun 12pm-7pm **CREDIT CARDS** visa, mastercard **MUNI** many

number 175 map G # CAFÉ FLORE

ADDRESS 2298 market @ noe **TELEPHONE** 621-8579 **OPENING HOURS** daily 7am-11pm **CREDIT CARDS** visa, mastercard **PRICE** $7 **MUNI** 24, 35, 37, f, k, l, m

On a warm, sunny day, it doesn't get much better than Café Flore. Loads of tables outside on the patio are still protected from any afternoon gusts of fog, and there are even more tables on the sidewalk in the really warm months. If you're lucky enough to get a spot, stay a while and make your way from lunch to cocktails to dinner. Even when it's not so warm and sunny, it's very pleasant to sit inside and sip coffee and try one of the many desserts.

ADDRESS 545 & 547 haight @ fillmore **TELEPHONE** grill 437-6851 pub 863-2276 **WEBSITE** www.toronado.com
OPENING HOURS grill daily 11:30am-10pm, pub daily 11:30am-2am **CREDIT CARDS** cash only **PRICE** $4
MUNI 6, 7, 22, 37, 66, 71, j, n

ROSAMUNDE SAUSAGE GRILL & TORONADO PUB number 176 map G

Polish sausages with hot and sweet peppers, sauerkraut and a Belgian Hoegaarden on tap … Is this Euro-backyard-BBQ heaven? No, it's Rosamunde Sausage Grill and Toronado Pub. Try a California-style sausage made with smoked chicken and cherries with a side of German potato salad, complemented by a fine California Boonville brew. The grill and bar are actually two separate businesses, but they're next door to each other and you're welcome to bring your brats over to the Toronado and watch some sports on their TVs, while enjoying one or more of their dozens of draught brews from all over the world.

The coffee, music and opera-singing waiters have made Caffe Trieste a North Beach hot spot since 1956. On a Saturday afternoon, what's better than enjoying an excellent espresso and some live opera? On your way out, pick up some freshly ground beans at the Annex.

ADDRESS 601 vallejo @ grant **TELEPHONE** 392-6739 **WEBSITE** www.caffetrieste.com **OPENING HOURS** sun-thu 6:30am-11pm, fri-sat 6:30am-midnight **CREDIT CARDS** none **PRICE** $4 **MUNI** 12, 15, 30, 45

number 177 map D

CAFFE TRIESTE

A "Prescription Pale Ale" sounds like the research and development team had a few drinks with the marketing team. Magnolia brews its own on location in this bright and airy corner of the Haight. From "Sara's Ruby Mild" to "Weather Report Wheat", your only worry will be how to figure out the bus map to get home. Whatever you get, add some house-cut French fries – four out of five doctors probably wouldn't recommend this, but that fifth guy has probably been to Magnolia's.

MAGNOLIA
PUB & BREWERY number 178 map D

ADDRESS 1398 haight @ masonic **TELEPHONE** 864-7468 **WEBSITE** www.magnoliapub.com **OPENING HOURS** mon-thu 12pm-midnight, fri 12pm-1am, sat 10am-1am, sun 10am-midnight **CREDIT CARDS** visa, mastercard, amex **PRICE** $11 **MUNI** 6, 7, 37, 43, 66, 71

number 179 map F **VESUVIO'S**

ADDRESS 255 columbus @ broadway **TELEPHONE** 362-3370 **WEBSITE** www.vesuvio.com **OPENING HOURS** daily 6am-2am **CREDIT CARDS** none **PRICE** $5 **MUNI** 12, 15, 30, 45, 83

Relive the beat revolution right at the spot where it all happened – or at least where the beats had drinks. Just getting through the photo history plastered on every wall will take you through a couple of cold pints of Anchor Steam. Or sample "The Jack Kerouac" with rum, tequila, orange and cranberry juices. If you can get an upstairs corner table, you'll have a window onto the world of North Beach. Enjoy your brew and let the history seep through your pores.

HOTEL BOHÈME number 180 map D

ADDRESS 444 columbus @ vallejo **TELEPHONE** 433-9111 **WEBSITE** www.hotelboheme.com **CREDIT CARDS** visa, mastercard, amex **PRICE** from $164 **MUNI** 12, 15, 30, 45

You're not going to get much more central than this. Right on Columbus, you'll have restaurants at your doorstep and cozy rooms if you don't want to go out at all. Soft colors and attention to detail make this a very easy place to stay. Gorgeous photography by Jerry Stahl lines the walls, all of it from the North Beach area in the 50s. Allen Ginsberg's favorite room was 204. Maybe they'll give you a deal if you want to stay more than a year …

With rooms called "The Flower Child" and "The Summer of Love," you might wonder whether you've stepped into a hotel, a museum or a time warp. In fact, you may have done all three. The Red Vic was at the center of the Peace Movement in the late 1960s. In 1977, Sami Sunchild dedicated herself to preserving this historic landmark as a "living museum." The 18-room hotel was built in 1904 as a country resort, back when this part of town was in the country. Continental breakfast is included and is a potentially interesting start to your day, as you might just sit next to someone else who was as intrigued as you were to step inside and go back in time.

number 181 map D **RED VICTORIAN**

ADDRESS 1665 haight @ cole **TELEPHONE** 864-1978 **WEBSITE** www.redvic.com **CREDIT CARDS** visa, mastercard, amex **PRICE** from $86 **MUNI** 6, 7, 33, 43, 66, 71

Colors are everywhere at this downtown hotel: there's the red bar, the blue café and the rainbow of ocean blues and soft yellows in the lobby. The hotel was built in the 1920s for merchant seamen passing through town and luxury-liner details are everywhere. This is no stuffy cruise line, however; it's a young, downtown favorite for travelers. Start your day with breakfast at the Titanic Café and finish it off with a cocktail at the (very) Red Room.

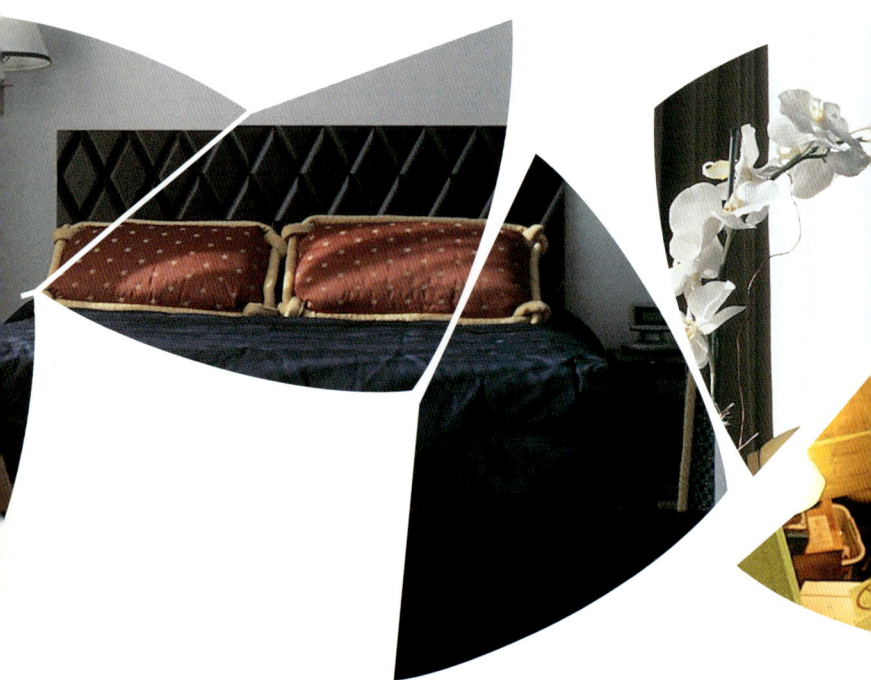

COMMODORE HOTEL number 182 map F

ADDRESS 825 sutter @ jones **TELEPHONE** 923-6800 **WEBSITE** www.thecommodorehotel.com
CREDIT CARDS visa, mastercard, amex **PRICE** from $89 **MUNI** 2, 3, 4, 27, 38

ADDRESS 2237 mason @ chestnut **TELEPHONE** 776-8688 **WEBSITE** www.sanremohotel.com **CREDIT CARDS** visa, mastercard, amex **PRICE** from $55 **MUNI** 15, 30, 39

number 183 map C # SAN REMO

You could buy a two-bedroom condo in this neighborhood for over a million dollars or stay at the San Remo and wake up to the same cappuccino café down the street. A few quieter blocks away from the main Columbus Avenue drag, you'll live more like a local in these North Beach Italianate Victorian digs. Claw-footed tubs, pull-chain toilets and shared bathrooms are all part of the old world charm of the San Remo.

CRUISIN' THE CASTRO number 184 map G

ADDRESS tour begins castro @ market **TELEPHONE** 550-8110 **WEBSITE** www.webcastro.com/castrotour
OPENING HOURS tue-sat 10am-2pm by reservation only, call or email trvrhailey@aol.com **CREDIT CARDS** none **PRICE** $40, including lunch **MUNI** 35, 37, 48, f, k, l, m

Walking around the Castro on your own is a tour in itself – even if you live there. But like most interesting spots, you don't know why it's interesting until someone tells you. Trevor Hailey has been telling people about the how, why, when and who of the Castro district since 1989. Take a walk on the wilder side with someone who can actually answer your questions.

From the recent stars of Sunday's funny papers, like Calvin and Hobbes, to the celebrities from the 1920s, such as Krazy Kat, the Cartoon Art Museum pays tribute to an all-American pastime – cartoons and comics. You're bound to recognize many of these faces, but you'll also see underground comics, graphic novels and animation. Many visitors enjoy the workshops and classes, where you get to try your own hand at this unique art form. Check the website for details.

number 185 map D **CARTOON ART MUSEUM**

ADDRESS 655 mission @ 3rd street **TELEPHONE** 227-8666 **WEBSITE** www.cartoonart.org **OPENING HOURS** tue-sun 11am-5pm **CREDIT CARDS** visa, mastercard **PRICE** $6 **MUNI** 6, 7, 9, 12, 14, 15, 21, f, j, k, l, m, n, bart: montgomery st

THE MARINA TRIANGLE

"The Triangle" got its name from three of the city's most popular bars that were all on the same corner - Fillmore at Greenwich. There are still three bars on that corner, but the **Balboa Café** is the only one that's original – since since 1914.

Professionals in their mid-20s and 30s – and those who'd like to fit into that category – party and live in **the Marina**. After the Marina-flattening-earthquake of 1989, some older folks moved out, rents went down and a wave of 90s dot-commers moved in. This is a clean-cut, affluent part of town – exactly the reason residents of other parts of town poke fun at it. If you live here, it's hard to complain about the **easy bay access, miles of jogging** and **bike lanes**, views all over the place, **unique shopping, upscale restaurants** and **trendy bars** and clubs. It's certainly different than other parts of town, and it's sometimes hard to believe that the Haight and the Marina are both parts of the same city, but that's what makes San Francisco so special.

Earthquakes have played an important role in the Marina. After the 1906 quake, fallen buildings and rubble from downtown were brought over to the north side of town and dumped into the marshlands there. Wanting to show the world how well it had recovered from the devastation, San Francisco hosted the **Pan-Pacific International Exhibition** in 1915. For the show, the city dumped more dirt and bricks on top of the marsh and added 30 blocks to the city. After the Expo, the temporary buildings were demolished (except for the Palace of Fine Arts, which was rebuilt in 1962), and San Francisco got some **prime beachfront property**. Thus, the Marina district was born.

There is actually a marina here, and when you see the **sailboats** heading out into the bay or a fleet of boats with people learning to sail, you get the sense that this is a **vacation** town. Squint your eyes and it could be Sydney or the French Riviera, but one thing is for sure: someone is having a good time.

The Marina boasts much of the city's greenery – **Crissy Field, Marina Green** and the vast forest of **The Presidio**. The Presidio alone is home to a golf course, a fun-filled museum (the Exploratorium), a lake, a pet cemetery and a nude beach. Crissy Field was recently transformed from an airstrip to a restored tidal marsh complete with sand dunes and a rolling, strolling promenade. Marina Green is a favorite of joggers, bicyclists, parents with strollers, roller-bladers, dogs, kites and Frisbees.

The green areas and history are wonderful, but when the dogs are on the leash and the roller-blades are in the closet, the Marina is still one of the best spots in the city for **eating, drinking** and **shopping**.

The heart of the shopping and restaurant scene spreads out from that legendary triangle on Fillmore. **Union Street** (aka Cow Hollow) goes east from Fillmore and **Chestnut Street** heads west. Walk east along Chestnut from Divisadero and you'll lose track of time in all the shops. When you get to **Cozmo's** on the corner, turn right and head up Fillmore to Union for shops, boutiques, jewelers, furniture stores, housewares and loads of eating options. Union Street is the more 'boutiquey' of the two streets, whereas Chestnut has more national brand shops.

There aren't many trees in the flat residential parts of the Marina, the ground isn't all that secure for the next earthquake and rent and home prices make much of the rest of the city look like a bargain basement, but you don't hear locals complaining too much.

THE MARINA TRIANGLE

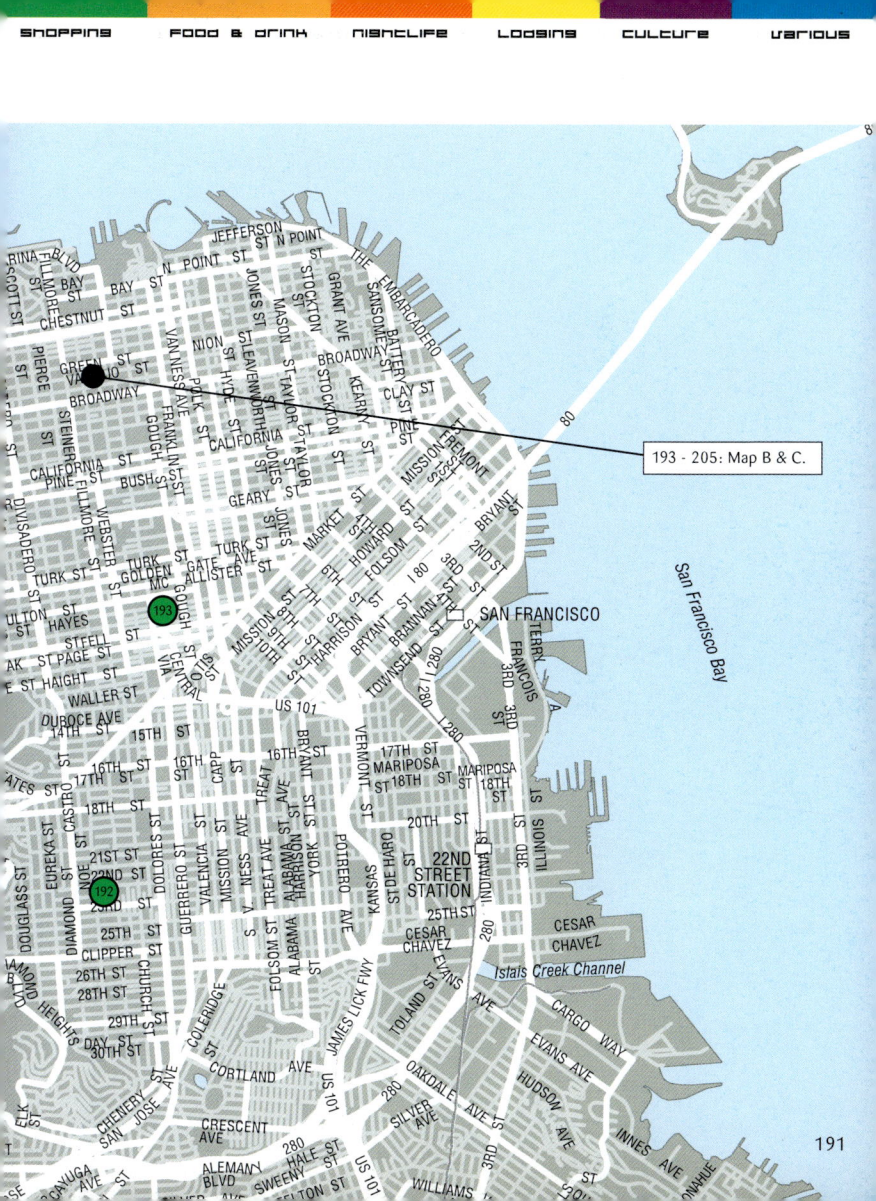

With both day- and evening-wear from designers such as Sue Wong, Betsy Johnson, BCBG Girls and Franco Sarto, Ambiance is like a mini-department store. Sue Wong mixes embroidery, floral patterns and beads to create a style that works for casual and formal events. The racks are packed with dresses and the shop is full of fashion-hungry women. The store's owners keep an eye on the fashion scene to make sure their selections are up-to-date, if not ahead of the curve.

AMBIANCE number 192 map C, F, G

ADDRESS three locations (1) 1864 union @ laguna (2) 1458 haight @ masonic (3) 3985 24th street @ noe
TELEPHONE 923-9797 **OPENING HOURS** daily 11am-7pm **CREDIT CARDS** visa, mastercard, amex **MUNI** (1) 41, 45 (2) 6, 37, 43 (3) 24, 48, j

number 193 map B, C **NIDA**

ADDRESS two locations (1) 2163 union @ fillmore (2) 544 hayes @ octavia **TELEPHONE** (1) 928-4670 (2) 552-4670 **WEBSITE** www.nidaboutique.com **OPENING HOURS** mon-sat 11am-7pm, sun 12pm-6pm **CREDIT CARDS** visa, mastercard, amex **MUNI** (1) 22, 45 (2) 5, 6, 7, 21, 47, 49, 71

These two San Francisco locations get most of their goods from Italy, but customize what they carry according to the neighborhood. For the Hayes Valley crowd, the stock is hip and urban. For the Marina woman, it's chic and tailored. Find the location that suits you best and be sure to check out the popular collection of bags.

This store is so casual and inviting that your friends can sit on comfy chairs and sip drinks while you model the latest from Buoy, Katayone Adeli, Rebecca Taylor and Chip and Pepper. Aside from clothing, there is an assortment of shoes, funky bags, belts and a small section for men. Get on the mailing list to be the first to hear about special sales, trunk shows and other in-the-know news.

RILEY JAMES number 194 map B, C

ADDRESS 3027 fillmore @ union **TELEPHONE** 775-7956 **OPENING HOURS** mon-sat 11am-8pm, sun 12pm-6pm
CREDIT CARDS visa, mastercard, amex **MUNI** 22, 45

number 195 map B, C # SUMBODY

ADDRESS 2167 union @ fillmore **TELEPHONE** 775-6343 **WEBSITE** www.sumbody.com **OPENING HOURS** mon-fri 10:30am-7pm, sat 10:30am-8pm, sun 10:30am-6pm **CREDIT CARDS** visa, mastercard **MUNI** 22, 45

Vanilla pudding and chocolate orange sounds delicious, as does pumpkin pie and hot chocolate... But if you're ready to unwrap one of these delights and pop it in your mouth, think again. You'll have to wait until you get home and plop it in your tub instead. These fresh, handmade and chemical-free scrubs and bath beads are made in a local workshop in Sebastopol. "A lot of people want to eat them," the shopkeeper says, "but they don't taste great."

BETELNUT PEJIU WU number 196 map B, C

ADDRESS 2030 union @ buchanan **TELEPHONE** 929-8855 **WEBSITE** www.betelnutrestaurant.com **OPENING HOURS** mon-thu 11:30am-11pm, sat-sun 11:30am-midnight **CREDIT CARDS** visa, mastercard **PRICE** $15 **MUNI** 22, 45

If oven-smoked sea bass with hints of ginger and cucumber and slowly waving palms on the ceiling sound like a relaxing evening to you, you might want to try this restaurant. Old-style posters line the deep-red walls above and stylish people line the walls below. This place was voted the "Hottest Restaurant in the Country" by the Boston Globe newspaper.

After a long night of reveling, you might feel like you could use something warm in your belly before you head home. As you step inside Pizza Orgasmica you'll know your worries are over. Try the "Ecstasy" with white wine cream sauce, or the "Girl from Ipanema" with Brazilian chicken. But don't take too much time deciding, because they close at 2am.

number 197 map B, C **PIZZA ORGASMICA**

ADDRESS 3157 fillmore @ greenwich **TELEPHONE** 931-5300 **WEBSITE** www.pizzaorgasmica.com **OPENING HOURS** sun-wed 11am-midnight, thu-sat 11am-2am **CREDIT CARDS** visa, mastercard, amex **PRICE** medium $14
MUNI 22, 30, 43, 46, 76

This place knows how to balance: the menu has old favorites as well as fresh innovation and the clients are a mix of old and young, singles and couples, well-dressed professionals and late-night pick-up scene types. Go with a classic like New York steak and have your choice of 25 wines by the glass. You can also enjoy some of the best burgers in town.

ADDRESS 3199 fillmore @ greenwich **TELEPHONE** 921-3944 **WEBSITE** www.plumpjack.com/pjbalboa
OPENING HOURS sun-wed 11:30am-10pm, thu-sat 11:30am-11pm, bar daily until 2am **CREDIT CARDS** visa, mastercard, amex **PRICE** $16 **MUNI** 22, 28, 30, 41, 45

BALBOA CAFÉ number 198 map B, C

ACE WASABI'S ROCK 'N' ROLL SUSHI

number 199 map B, C

ADDRESS 3339 steiner @ chestnut **TELEPHONE** 567-4903 **WEBSITE** www.acewasabis.com **OPENING HOURS** mon-thu 5:30pm-10:30pm, fri-sat 5:30pm-11pm, sun 5pm-10pm **CREDIT CARDS** visa, mastercard, amex **PRICE** $12 **MUNI** 28, 30, 43, 76

At Ace Wasabi, blaring music flows onto the street each time the door opens. The DJ and hip tunes are extremely inviting. Once you're in, you'll stay to enjoy specialty dishes like the Flying Kamikaze Roll with asparagus wrapped with albacore tuna, topped with ponzu and scallions or perhaps partake in the weekday game of Bingo nightly at 6:30pm. In the Marina, this is the place to see and be seen.

MATRIXFILLMORE number 200 map B, C

ADDRESS 3138 fillmore @ greenwich **TELEPHONE** 563-4180 **WEBSITE** www.plumpjack.com/pjmatrix
OPENING HOURS daily 5:30pm-2am **CREDIT CARDS** visa, mastercard, amex **PRICE** $8, no cover **MUNI** 22, 30, 43, 46, 76

MatrixFillmore is as hip as they come, with its soft velvet seating along the felt walls, a modern fireplace that merits a double-take and lighting that's just bright enough to catch the wink of an eye. Marty Balin opened The Matrix in 1965 so his new band would have a place to play. On opening night, his band was named Jefferson Airplane. MatrixFillmore has even put out a CD of their "Deep Lounge" tunes called MATRIXFILLMOREONE. While you're there, try a PearUp, consisting of pear puree, apple juice and vodka.

shopping   food & drink   nightlife   lodging   culture   various

The crowd at Comet Club is local on weekdays and on weekends what they call "bridge and tunnel". Playing jazz, acid jazz, raregroove, lounge, classic 70s and 80s house, funk and groove, the Comet Club is young and high energy. The music is loud, so bring your dancing shoes or just enjoy happy hour with $2.50 beers and mixed drinks (Tue-Sun 7pm-10pm). There's a dress code on Saturday and Sunday after 9pm.

number 201 map B, C **COMET CLUB**

ADDRESS 3111 fillmore @ filbert **TELEPHONE** 567-5589 **OPENING HOURS** tue-wed 7pm-2am, thu-sat 5:30pm-2am **CREDIT CARDS** visa, mastercard **PRICE** $5 **MUNI** 22, 41, 45

At most times, Mauna Loa is pretty low-key. There's a pool table, some foosball (table soccer) games and some small TVs to catch the Giants game. You might, however, just prefer to sit near the window and watch the Fillmore cruisers. Whether you're in with the after-work drinks crowd and old-school locals blowing off some steam on a weeknight or with the Marina crowds on weekends, Mauna Loa is unpretentious. It's pretty hard to be pretentious with a bar covered in parquet wood, but maybe that's what has kept people coming here since 1939.

MAUNA LOA CLUB number 202 map B, C

ADDRESS 3009 fillmore @ union **TELEPHONE** 563-5137 **OPENING HOURS** mon-fri 2pm-2am, sat-sun 12pm-2am **CREDIT CARDS** cash only **MUNI** 22, 41, 45

number 203 map B, C **HOTEL DRISCO**

ADDRESS 2901 pacific @ broderick **TELEPHONE** 346-2880 **WEBSITE** www.hoteldrisco.com **CREDIT CARDS** visa, mastercard, amex **PRICE** from $150 **MUNI** 3, 24

If you're not looking out for this hotel, you'll likely miss it – which is just fine with its Pacific Heights neighbors. See what it's like to live in one of the city's ritziest and glitziest neighborhoods, at least for a night or two. The rooms are just what you would hope for: lush, plush and not in a rush. The higher floors provide views normally only seen in postcards. Enjoy it while it lasts.

HOTEL DEL SOL number 204 map B, C

ADDRESS 3100 webster @ greenwich **TELEPHONE** 921-5520 **WEBSITE** www.thehoteldelsol.com
CREDIT CARDS visa, mastercard, amex **PRICE** from $129 **MUNI** 22, 28, 43, 76

Transformed from a 50s-style motor lodge into a bright and cheery California beach motel, the Hotel Del Sol is at the heart of the Marina District's shopping and nightlife. It's also just a leisurely walk or rollerblade away from the Marina Green and Crissy Field, two of San Francisco's bayside green expanses. It does have one aspect that is very un-San Francisco, though: free parking.

shopping　　Food & Drink　　nightlife　　Lodging　　culture　　various

This place feels like a home because it is a home. With only six rooms, you and your fellow guests practically become a family, but the rooms are private and you don't have to share your marmalade if you'd rather not. Head back to the gardens, where there is so much green that it's hard to believe you're right at the doorstep of the Marina district's shopping, restaurants and nightlife.

number 205 map B, C **UNION STREET INN**

ADDRESS 2229 union @ fillmore **TELEPHONE** 346-0424 **WEBSITE** www.unionstreetinn.com **CREDIT CARDS** visa, mastercard, amex **PRICE** from $169, breakfast included **MUNI** 22, 41, 45

From a military airstrip in the 1920s to an abandoned asphalt jungle to a pleasant, grassy environmentally protected area, Crissy Field has come full circle. Walk, bike, Frisbee, jog, blade, sailboard, fly kites or just sit and enjoy the ocean breezes and the view of the bay and Golden Gate Bridge. Twenty acres of original tidal marshland have been restored and are now protected from further development. If the famous fog rolls in, warm up with a hot drink at the Warming Hut.

CRISSY FIELD number 206 map A

ADDRESS between golden gate bridge and the marina district **TELEPHONE** 561-7690 **WEBSITE** www.crissyfield.org **MUNI** 28, 29, 43

OVERVIEW MAP SAN FRANCISCO

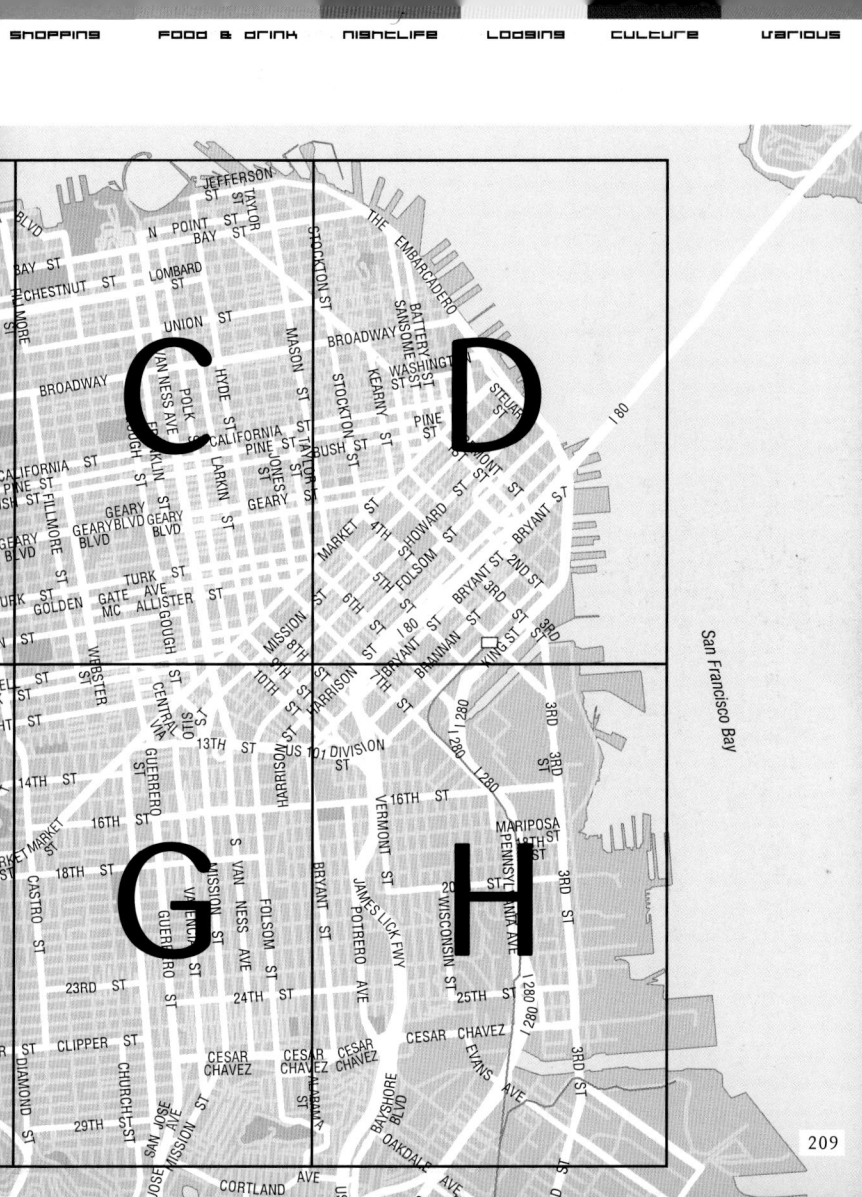

MAP A

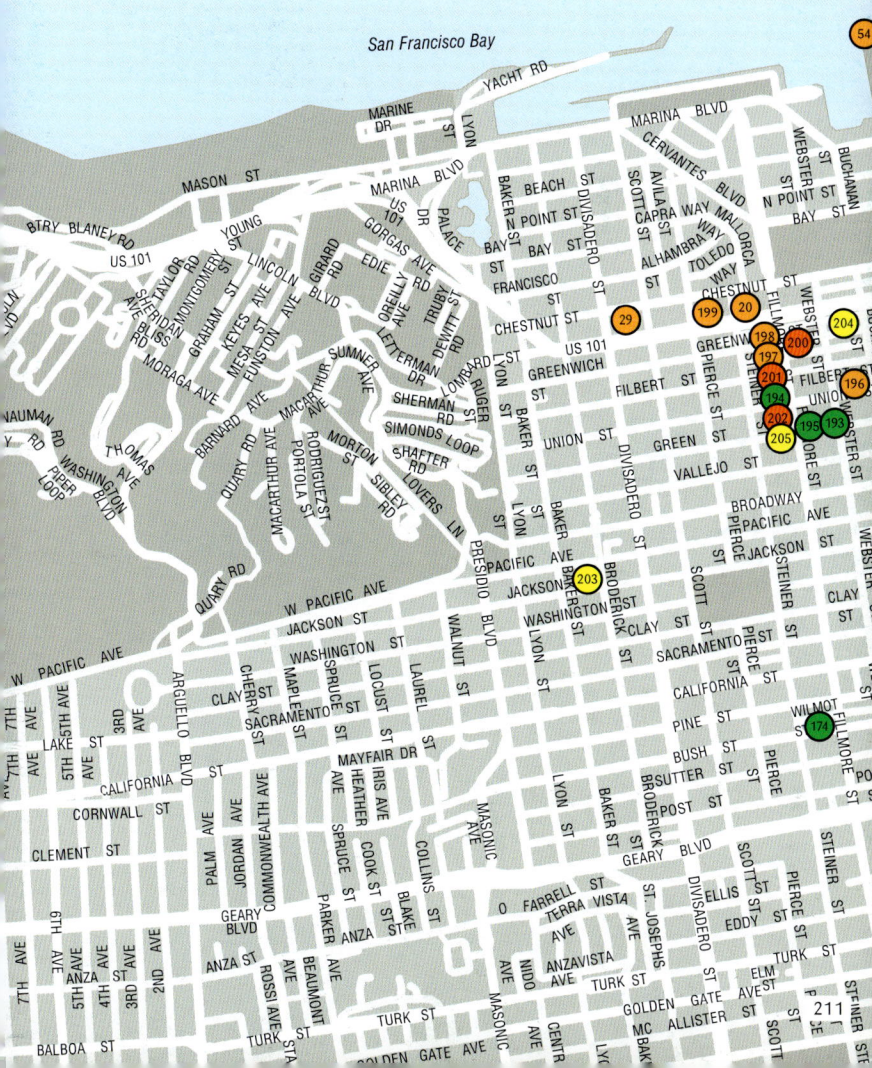

MAP B

MAP C

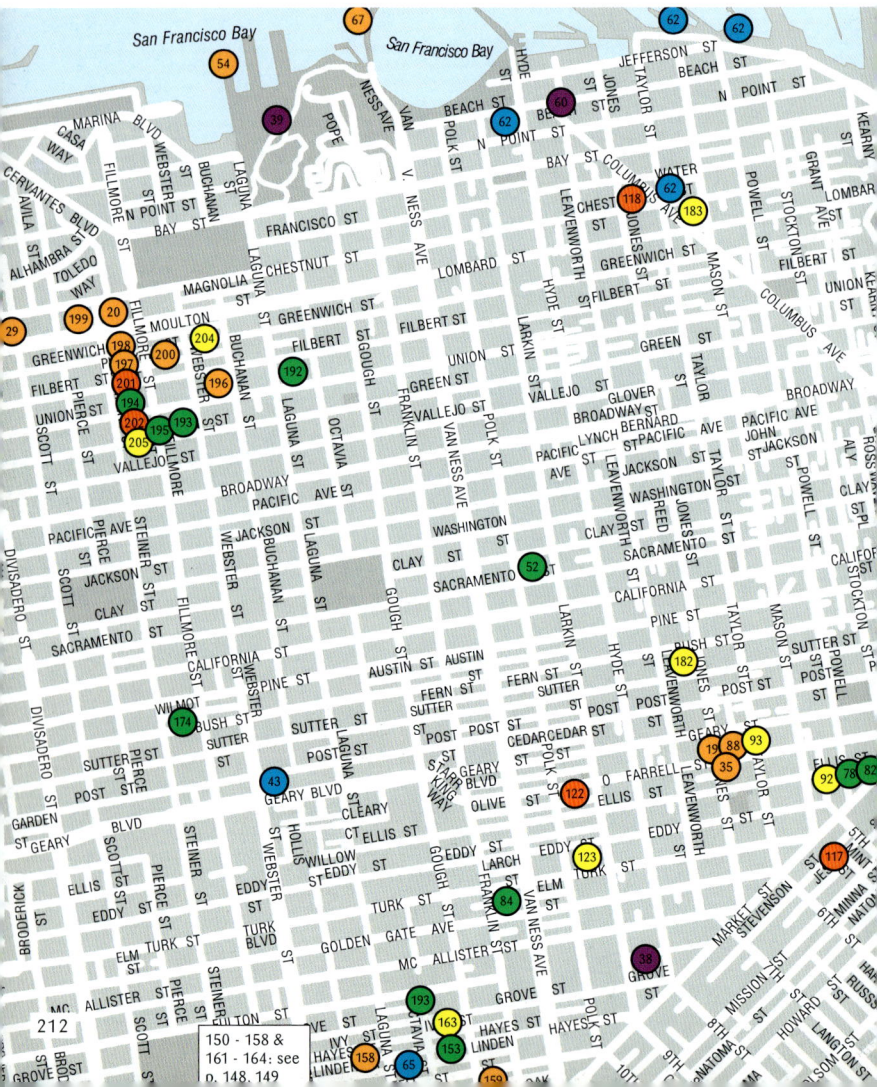

MAP D

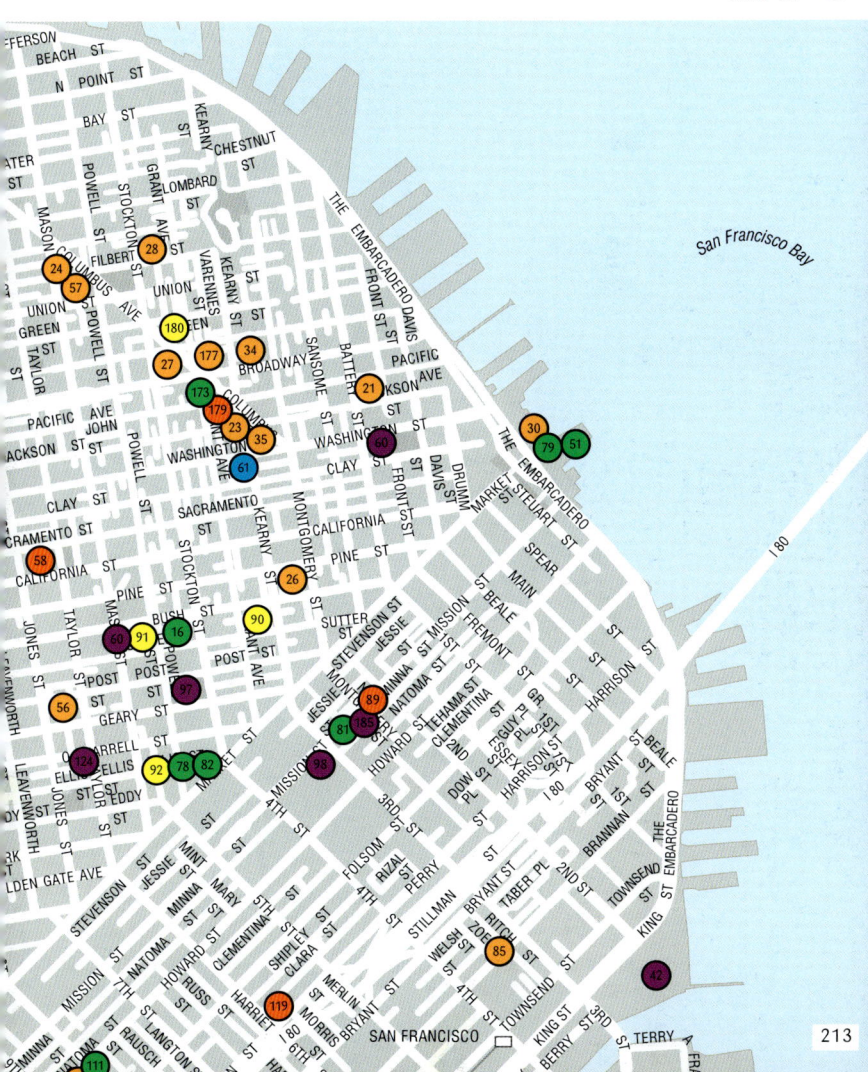

MAP E

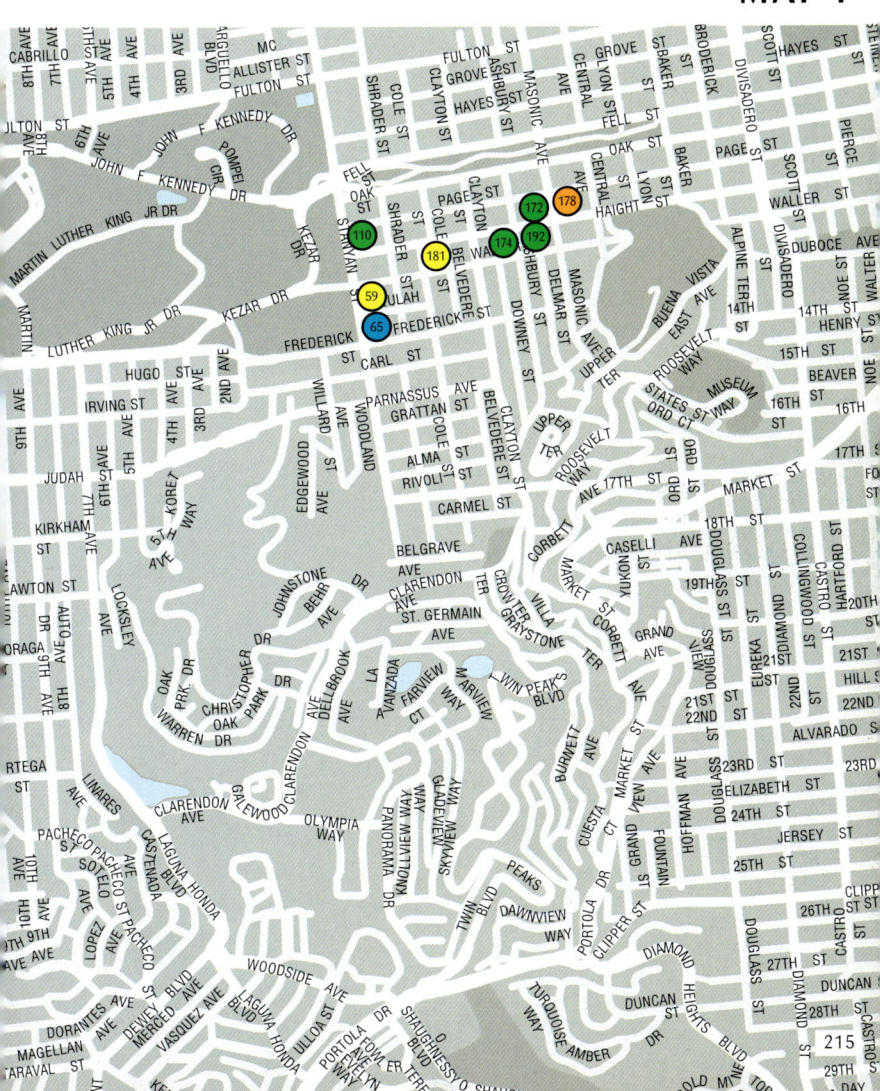

MAP G

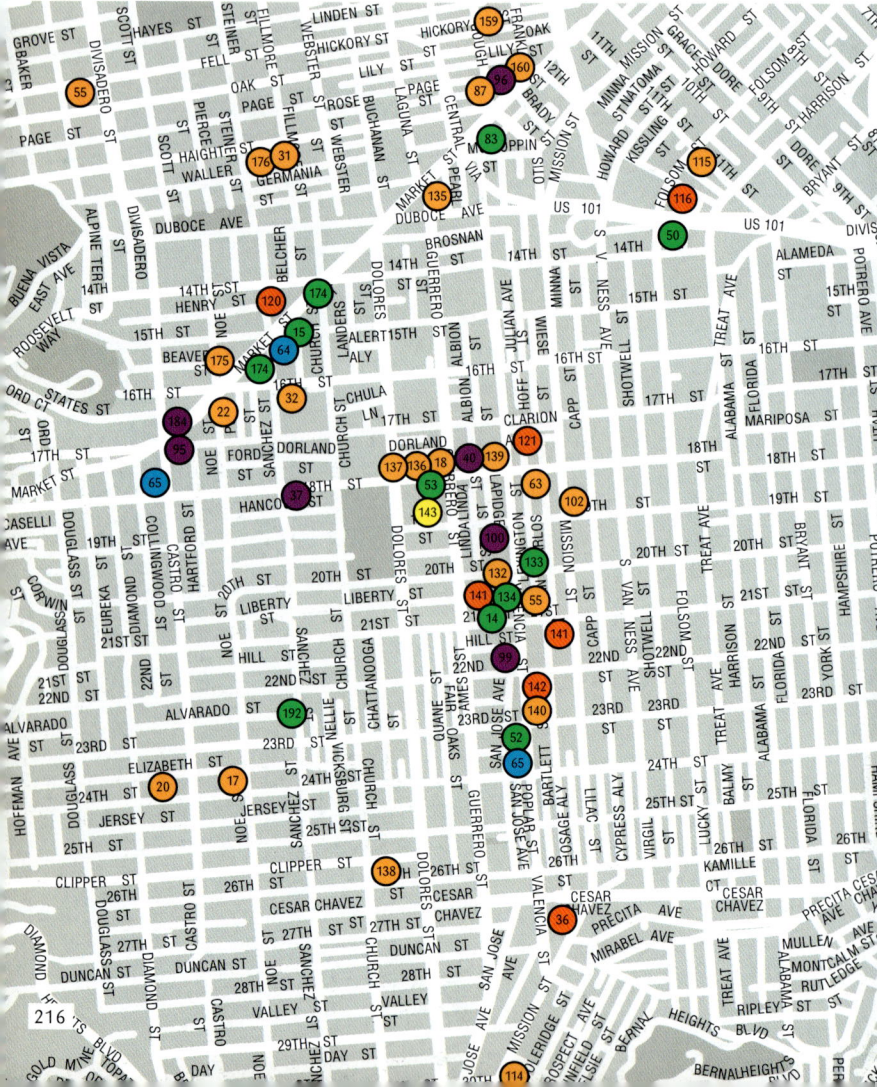

MAP H

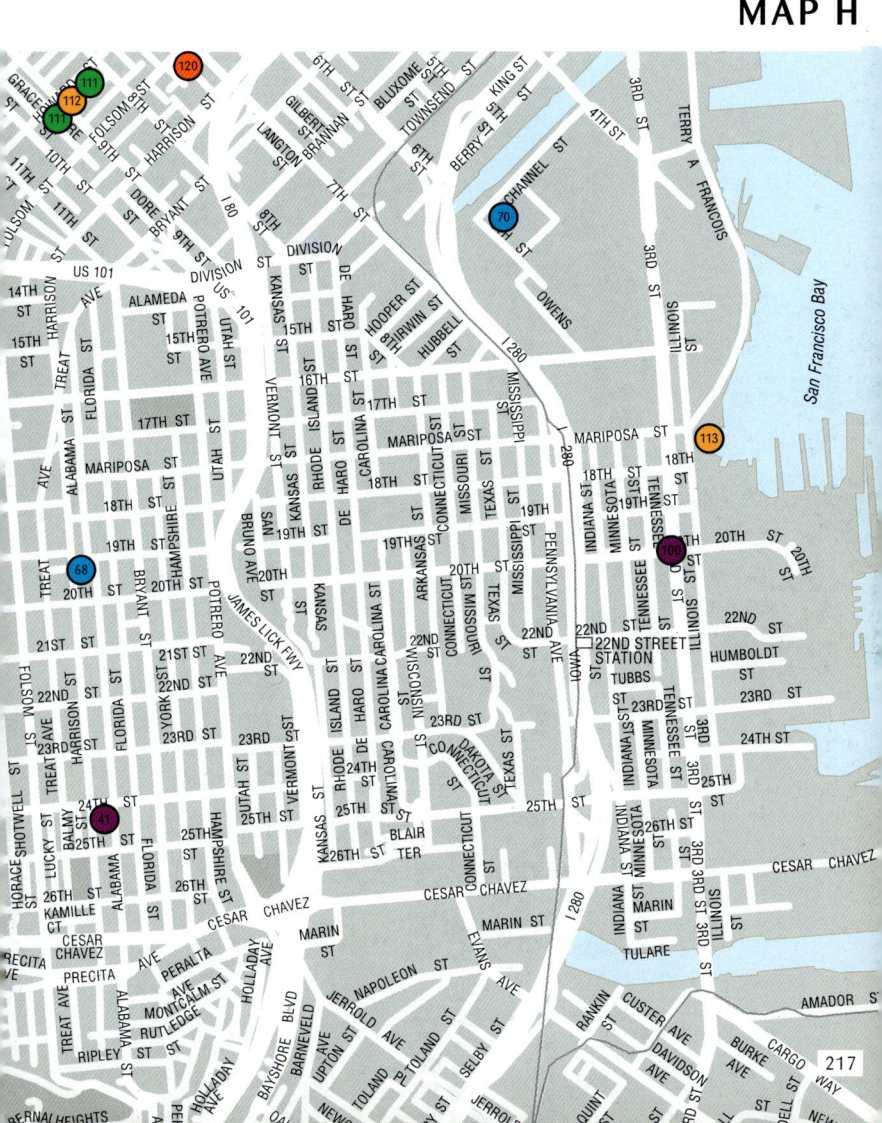

CATEGORY INDEX

CULTURE
66balmy	40
asian art museum	38
cartoon art museum	185
castro theatre	95
city art	100
city guides	94
cruisin' the castro	184
fort mason	39
glide memorial church	124
karma moffett's tibetan bell ceremony	37
laughter, the best medicine	60
linc	96
marsh, the	99
pacbell park	42
precita eyes mural tours	41
tix	97
yerba buena center for the arts	98

FOOD & DRINK
ace wasabi's rock 'n' roll sushi	199
asiasf	112
bacar	85
balboa café	198
barney's gourmet hamburgers	20
belden place	26
betelnut pejiu wu	196
café flore	175
café marimba	29
cafe tartine	159
caffe trieste	177
canvas	86
da flora	24
delfina	137
dottie's true blue café	19
emmy's spaghetti shack	114
frjtz	162
grand café	88
greens	54
helmand, the	34
herbivore	55
hotel biron	87
house of nanking	23
indian oven	31
juicey lucy's	57
kokkari estiatorio	21
last supper club	140
liguria bakery	28
lovejoy's tea room	138
luna park	139
magnolia pub & brewery	178
millennium	56
molinari delicatessen	27
naan 'n curry	35
pizza orgasmica	197
place pigalle	161
platanos	18
ramp, the	113
rosamunde sausage grill & toronado pub	176
slanted door, the	30
suppenküche	158
sushi groove south	115
tangerine	32
tartine bakery	136
tin pan	22
ton kiang	33
zante pizza & indian cuisine	25
zeitgeist	135
zuni café	160

LODGING
clift	93
commodore hotel	182
hayes valley inn	163
hotel bohème	180
hotel del sol	204
hotel drisco	203
hotel rex	91
hotel triton	90
hotel tropicana	143
monticello inn	92
phoenix hotel	123
red victorian	181
san remo	183
stanyan park hotel	59
union street inn	205

NIGHTLIFE
111 minna	89
bimbo's 365 club	118
café du nord	120
comet club	201
el rio	36
elbo room	121
endup, the	119
foreign cinema	141
grace after hours	58
great american music hall	122
make-out room	142
matrixfillmore	200
mauna loa club	202
mezzanine	117
vesuvio's	179
wish	116

SHOPPING

alabaster	150
alla prima	152
ambiance	192
amoeba music	110
anthropologie	82
barking frog, the	15
bi-rite	53
book passage	79
bulo	153
buu	156
city lights bookstore	173
clean well-lighted place for books	84
crossroads trading company	174
encantada	14
ferry plaza farmer's market	51
flax art & design	83
flight 001	154
global exchange	17
good vibrations	52
kar'ikter	16
lava 9	155
nida	193
piedmont boutique	172
propeller	151
rainbow grocery co-op	50
retro fit vintage	134
riley james	194
rolo	111
sfmoma museumstore	81
subterranean shoe room	133
sumbody	195
urban outfitters	78
velvet da vinci	157
wishbone	80
x21	132

VARIOUS

2202 oxygen bar	63
angel island	67
blazing saddles	62
crissy field	206
gallery spanganga	102
kabuki springs & spa	43
lindy in the park	125
mission bay golf center	70
mission cliffs	68
nickel spa	64
open houses	101
oxenrose	164
presidio golf course	69
skating in the park	66
trū	61
yoga tree	65

ALPHABETICAL INDEX

111 minna	89
2202 oxygen bar	63
66balmy	40

A
ace wasabi's rock 'n' roll sushi	199
alabaster	150
alla prima	152
ambiance	192
amoeba music	110
angel island	67
anthropologie	82
asian art museum	38
asiasf	112

B
bacar	85
balboa café	198
barking frog, the	15
barney's gourmet hamburgers	20
belden place	26
betelnut pejiu wu	196
bimbo's 365 club	118
biron, hotel	87
bi-rite	53
blazing saddles	62
bohème, hotel	180
book passage	79
bulo	153
buu	156

C
café du nord	120
café flore	175
café marimba	29
café tartine	159
caffe trieste	177
canvas	86
cartoon art museum	185
castro theatre	95
city art	100
city guides	94
city lights bookstore	173
clean well-lighted place for books	84
clift	93
comet club	201
commodore hotel	182
crissy field	206
crossroads trading company	174
cruisin' the castro	184

D
da flora	24
del sol, hotel	204
delfina	137
dottie's true blue café	19
drisco, hotel	203

E
el rio	36
elbo room	121
emmy's spaghetti shack	114
encantada	14
endup, the	119

F
ferry plaza farmer's market	51
flax art & design	83
flight 001	154
foreign cinema	141
fort mason	39
frjtz	162

G
gallery spanganga	102
glide memorial church	124
global exchange	17
good vibrations	52
grace after hours	58
grand café	88
great american music hall	122
greens	54

H
hayes valley inn	163
helmand, the	34
herbivore	55
house of nanking	23

I
indian oven	31

J
juicey lucy's	57

K
kabuki springs & spa	43
kar'ikter	16
karma moffett's tibetan bell ceremony	37
kokkari estiatorio	21

L

last supper club	140
laughter, the best medicine	60
lava 9	155
liguria bakery	28
linc	96
lindy in the park	125
lovejoy's tea room	138
luna park	139

M

magnolia pub & brewery	178
make-out room	142
marsh, the	99
matrixfillmore	200
mauna loa club	202
mezzanine	117
millennium	56
mission bay golf center	70
mission cliffs	68
molinari delicatessen	27
monticello inn	92

N

naan 'n curry	35
nickel spa	64
nida	193

O

open houses	101
oxenrose	164

P

pacbell park	42
phoenix hotel	123
piedmont boutique	172
pizza orgasmica	197
place pigalle	161
platanos	18
precita eyes mural tours	41
presidio golf course	69
propeller	151

R

rainbow grocery co-op	50
ramp, the	113
red victorian	181
retro fit vintage	134
rex, hotel	91
riley james	194
rolo	111
rosamunde sausage & toronado pub	176

S

san remo	183
sfmoma museumstore	81
skating in the park	66
slanted door, the	30
stanyan park hotel	59
subterranean shoe room	133
sumbody	195
suppenküche	158
sushi groove south	115

T

tangerine	32
tartine bakery	136
tin pan	22
tix	97
ton kiang	33
triton, hotel	90
tropicana, hotel	143
trū	61

U

union street inn	205
urban outfitters	78

V

velvet da vinci	157
vesuvio's	179

W

wish	116
wishbone	80

X

x21	132

Y

yerba buena center for the arts	98
yoga tree	65

Z

zante pizza & indian cuisine	25
zeitgeist	135
zuni café	160

notes

notes

ALSO AVAILABLE

 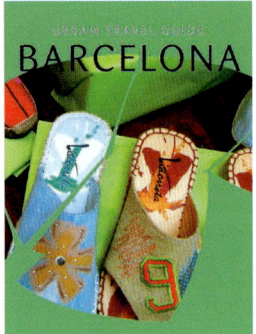 

URBAN TRAVEL GUIDE
PARIS
isbn 90-5767-125-5

URBAN TRAVEL GUIDE
BARCELONA
isbn 90-5767-128-x

URBAN TRAVEL GUIDE
LONDON
isbn 90-5767-127-1

TO BE RELEASED OCTOBER 2004

URBAN TRAVEL GUIDE
NEW YORK